The Art of Quantum Planning

Lessons from Quantum Physics for Breakthrough Strategy, Innovation, and Leadership

Gerald Harris

BK

Berrett–Koehler Publishers, Inc.
San Francisco
a BK Business book

Berrett-Koehler Publishers, Inc.
235 Montgomery Street, Suite 650
San Francisco, CA 94104-2916
Tel: (415) 288-0260   Fax: (415) 362-2512   www.bkconnection.com

Ordering Information

Quantity sales. Special discounts are available on quantity purchases by corporations, associations, and others. For details, contact the "Special Sales Department" at the Berrett-Koehler address above.

Individual sales. Berrett-Koehler publications are available through most bookstores. They can also be ordered directly from Berrett-Koehler: Tel: (800) 929-2929; Fax: (802) 864-7626; www.bkconnection.com

Orders for college textbook/course adoption use. Please contact Berrett-Koehler: Tel: (800) 929-2929; Fax: (802) 864-7626.

Orders by U.S. trade bookstores and wholesalers. Please contact Ingram Publisher Services, Tel: (800) 509-4887; Fax: (800) 838-1149; For details about online ordering, visit www.ingrampublisherservices.com/Ordering. E-mail correspondence can be addressed to customer.service@ingrampublisherservices.com.

Berrett-Koehler and the BK logo are registered trademarks of Berrett-Koehler Publishers, Inc.

Printed in the United States of America

Berrett-Koehler books are printed on long-lasting acid-free paper. When it is available, we choose paper that has been manufactured by environmentally responsible processes. These may include using trees grown in sustainable forests, incorporating recycled paper, minimizing chlorine in bleaching, or recycling the energy produced at the paper mill.

Library of Congress Cataloging-in-Publication Data

Harris, Gerald (Gerald Anthony)
        The art of quantum planning : lessons from quantum physics for breakthrough strategy, innovation, and leadership / Gerald Harris. -- 1st ed.
        p. cm.
    Includes bibliographical references and index.
    ISBN 978-1-60509-265-2 (alk. paper)
        1. Strategic planning. 2. Business planning. 3. Leadership. 4. Creative thinking.
    5. Quantum theory. I. Title.
    HD30.28.H3735 2009
    658.4'01--dc22   2009020967

First Edition
14 13 12 11 10 09   10 9 8 7 6 5 4 3 2 1

Project management, design, and composition by Dovetail Publishing Services

This book is dedicated to my sons, Brandon and Corbin, and my daughters by marriage, Kena and Kai. I hope it inspires them all to reach for their full potential.

Contents

Acknowledgements

I OWE MUCH GRATITUDE TO MANY PEOPLE who over my lifetime have been very supportive and encouraging. I have found in my life that the people who love and care for me often see more capability in me than I initially see in myself. With their encouragement, I have stretched further and accomplished a lot—writing this book being a prime example.

I begin with my lovely wife, Dr. Brenda Wade, who I watched work through her third book in 2006—wrestling both with the deep meditation that comes from the inside when writing, as well as the frustrating vagaries of computers, saving copies and emailing chapters for review. Once she was done, I have to say it gave me inspiration to try it one day myself. Without Brenda's steady and loving encouragement to share my ideas and to believe that other people would be interested, I doubt if I ever would have even got started.

Peter Schwartz, Napier Collyns, Jay Ogilvy and my colleagues at Global Business Network (GBN) have been vital to my whole world view. I learned so much from working with them that I believe my personal identity can't be separated from the experience. Meeting and working with Peter Schwartz was a positive pivot point in my life. Napier's encouragement, after reviewing the initial manuscript, gave me the energy to keep going and give the book my very best. The encouragement of Nancy Murphy and Lynn Carruthers throughout my years of practice at GBN taught me a lot about communicating from the heart. My brilliant GBN colleagues from Europe, Kees van der Heijden and Jaap Leemhuis, grounded my views on how to do effective strategic planning. I will be forever indebted to the whole GBN family.

The review and encouragement of John Renesch of the earliest manuscript was vital to keeping my energy up. John was a living angel when I needed one.

Finally, I am very thankful to Steve Piersanti, Jeevan Sivasubramaniam and the entire Berrett-Koehler staff for their support and encouragement. In particular, I thank Steve for coming back to me after I was initially very reluctant to take on a book. Working with Steve as the editor made this much less of a burden than I imagined. His clarity and direction were always on point. Jeevan's thoughtfulness was just what I needed to give the book a tighter focus. I look forward to being part of the Berrett-Koehler family in the years ahead.

Foreword

GERALD HARRIS IS A FRIEND AND COLLEAGUE of nearly 20 years of shared experience. His insightful book is based on that experience and his own creative learning. He applies a body of some of the most profound ideas of our time about how reality works to some of the most challenging problems facing organizations as they try to gain influence over their futures in the midst of a time of unprecedented uncertainty.

I have had the pleasure of working in scenario planning for 37 years in the world of consulting and in business. The most important experience was at the Royal Dutch Shell Group in London, where I headed their scenario planning group during the 1980s. I met Gerald a couple of years after a few friends and I started the Global Business Network and Pacific Gas and Electric became one of our first clients. He was then part of their strategic planning team. He showed such aptitude and interest in that work that he left PG&E to join us only a few years later.

In this new book Gerald has taken a very useful approach to gaining insight: applying novel ideas from one field, physics, to another, strategic planning, to see if they shed useful light on the problems of the latter. The important question is whether the realties of organizational strategic planning, similar to the realities described by quantum physics, not in a literal but metaphorical sense. Here is where intellectual horsepower and long experience come to bear. Gerald makes the case strongly for the utility of these ideas in the world of strategic planning and then proves it by successfully applying the ideas to many of the important problems and issues faced by strategic planners and thinkers.

Gerald's years of experience have provided him the same lesson that came from my Shell experience. The hardest challenge is not anticipating the future or devising a better strategy for that future. Rather it is changing the minds of decision makers, who are usually in their positions because of a long history of success. That success means they trust their own view and judgment and are not easily pointed in new directions. Successfully influencing that mind is not like the rational process of re-programming a machine as in the old mechanistic Newtonian paradigm. Rather, changing another's perception is a more subtle process like the fact that the observer determines the outcome by his act of measurement in quantum mechanics.

At the heart of both quantum physics and scenario planning is the problem of uncertainty, one in the physical world and the other in the mind of the decision maker. The art of the quantum planning applies the tools of one to shed useful light on the other. Planning as a dynamic learning process rather than a control process drives Gerald's thinking and again relies on the models of quantum uncertainty to clarify the issues for the strategic planner.

One after another, Gerald frames the challenges facing the strategic planner and then provides helpful and practical ways of addressing them with the tools of quantum thinking. This is perhaps only the beginning of a dialog with these ideas and both the reader, the wider planning community and Gerald will continue to carry them forward in dealing with ever greater complexity and uncertainty.

—*Peter Schwartz*
San Francisco

Planning, Thinking, and Learning

"Don't squeeze the club too tightly. Don't think about everything I told you; just play with it and swing. Let the feeling come to you."

These are some of the instructions given
to me on how to swing a golf club.

MY BOOKCASE HAS MANY GOOD BOOKS about business planning, strategy, and leadership. Many of them have served me well throughout my career as an executive and strategic planner both in a major corporation and as a management consultant. So what is it that would drive me to write another book on those subjects, and why should you take time to read it? The short answer is to address a failure that I have witnessed that has cost companies and organizations a great deal—the failure to think and plan in a more open, learning-oriented, and innovative manner.

What's Missing in Good Books on Strategic Planning?

I have seen a tendency to get stuck in old patterns, unhealthy group-think, and narrow safe zones. Certainly it is not for a lack of trying to break those tendencies that this failure has occurred. What has been missing in efforts to break free is a set of clear and well-grounded tools that can be relied on to spur innovative thinking and keep minds open to continuous learning. What is needed is something that can serve as a relatively easy-to-use tool to help managers, planners, and their teams "get out of the box," break through unhealthy or stale group-think, and reliably point to ways to give constructive challenges to what might be dangerous assumptions. This book is for people involved in planning the future of their organizations (from the top management down to individual contributors) who want sure-fire protection against narrow thinking and a quick, easy-to-use reference for some stimulating concepts to assure more innovative thinking.

Starting with my time at Pacific Gas and Electric Company as Director of Business Planning for the Engineering and Construction Unit, and throughout my fifteen years as a management consultant with Global Business Network, I have been involved with well over a hundred planning teams. I have led and participated in world-class planning, as well as some efforts that I thought were half-hearted. I have worked directly with CEOs and senior managers to help them develop key strategies for the future of their companies. In the best of those engagements, managers were dedicated to thinking and learning in an open way. I experienced a resistance to "locking down" and closing off ideas, and openness to contributions from a wide range of sources. I have not been able to "reverse-engineer" all of what I experienced, but I decided it would be useful to find some tools to generate the quality of thinking I was seeing. In my search I found the best ideas, surprisingly, in quantum physics! I will say more about this shortly.

Here are the problems I want to solve for you in this book:

1. You are about to start or lead, or are in the middle of, a
   strategic planning process for your organization and you want

to guard against doing "the same old thing" and coming up with "in-the-box," safe, and unchallenging results.

2. You want to have a reliable checklist at hand to help yourself, or possibly your team, avoid any unhealthy groupthink that might emerge.

3. You or your team have settled on your core facts, beliefs, stories, and related strategies, and there is little real innovation. You want a way to systematically and quickly revisit your results to generate more expansive thinking.

4. You are using scenarios in strategic planning, but you want high-quality wild cards and more challenging and innovative stories that might lead to more innovative strategic thinking.

Those four problems are ones I have continually encountered in my career. What I have created here is a book that addresses those problems by interpreting seven core ideas from what scientists are learning about how the universe works and translating them into ideas that can spur innovative thinking for planners.

This book is not for physicists or people who want to learn more about physics. (For the curious I include some references I have found useful.) It is for people who want to help their organizations grow and have better futures and who want great ideas to accomplish these goals in an innovative, strategic plan.

My core belief about what makes for quality strategic planning is to have a *learning-oriented* approach. Planning is a way for an organization to learn its way forward and compete more effectively by making quality decisions. I believe this based on my own experience and also from the advice of experts in the field whom I have been fortunate enough to work with and become friends with (Don Michael, Peter Schwartz, Kees van der Heijden, and Arie de Gues among them). Good strategic planning occurs in cycles, in some cases annually, but more often in two- to three-year increments (because it takes time to implement and get feedback from strategies pursued and actions taken). The integration of what has been learned through past actions and the efficiency of that process is the core of quality strategic planning.

Learning is a thinking process, so the quality of thinking is central. This book presents tools for thinking differently and in a more open and innovative manner. As the quality of thinking increases in an organization through using the tools presented in this book, I believe that the quality of the results will improve as well.

Leaders have a big role in the quality of thinking in their organizations. I see effective leaders as encouraging, creating an environment for friendly and rewarding high-quality thinking. I do not believe the role of a leader is to have all the good ideas and be the sole source of high-quality thinking. A single-person, star-based system of leadership cannot work in the complex business environments all organizations face today. I am advocating that leaders build organizational environments that encourage the use of the tools I set forth to generate higher quality thinking and innovative ideas. Chapter 1 provides more on my core ideas about good leadership and planning in organizations.

Now, you may ask, why use ideas from quantum physics? In my experience, they work and fit well. I also have found the concepts relatively easy to understand, and they translate into truly usable tools to expand my thinking and keep me open to learning more. I can see their direct application to the kind of planning processes I have led. Quantum physics is based on understanding reality as an integrated and wonderfully interconnected system. I see the business environments that organizations face as integrated and wonderfully interconnected systems as well, so translating ideas from physics to the business environment just might prove fruitful.

Physics is a complex subject. It is the science of matter and motion. There are many branches within physics itself: for example, astrophysics, which deals with the physical properties of the universe and the movement of planets, stars, galaxies, and the like, andr particle physics, which deals with the smallest particles of matter. The most intelligent and studied physicists approach the subject with awe, respect, and a burning curiosity (a reading of Walter Isaacson's biography of Albert Einstein makes this very clear.)

As a field of study, physics is full of fantastic ideas (e.g., the Big Bang Theory). The discoveries from physics are a powerful influence in the history of man leading to the creation of some the most wonderful products we enjoy in the modern world (such as the computer I am currently using to write this book). The ideas from physics have also found resonance in philosophy; the interconnectedness of all things is both a physical and a philosophical notion. The step I am taking is akin to finding parallels in the ideas emerging from physics that relate to those of philosophy. I am using them for the more practical tasks of spurring ideas through which we can better create and manage organizations. I want them to serve as pathways for challenging assumptions, inspiring new perspectives, and encouraging more open and learning-oriented thinking and planning. I am not the first person to draw from the work of physicists to try to get some value for the world of business. The mathematics behind the Fischer Black–Myron Scholes models in the world of finance that have led to modeling of risks and share-price movements in modern financial markets is derived from heat-diffusion models from physics.

I am willing to take the risk of not being as precise in my interpretation of the science as a trained physicist might required to reach for something that might be useful. To any physicists who happen upon this book (it is not for you) and beg to differ with my use of the ideas, my response will be, "Please tell me more."

Playing with the ideas is a good place to start. This brings me to my golf lesson alluded to in the opening display quote. I want to draw from that the attitude I would like you to approach in using the ideas of this book—that is, one of play. Playing is learning by doing, and while doing, being forgiving of mistakes as part of the learning process. A mistake is not failure, but a tool for calibrating and trying again. Playing is an interactive process between doing and thinking, and one's imagination.

I invite you to hold the ideas in your head lightly, understand my suggestions on the "how to," yet hold a space to learn by playing with the ideas and using your imagination. I think the twists and turns your brain may go through in pondering the ideas might best be captured with a playful attitude. There may be no "right way" to hold these ideas—just infinite combinations with which to play with them. When you feel you have it, then apply your maximum strengths and intellect. Chapter 2 provides more detail on the ideas.

The central chapters of this book are Chapters 3 through 9; they interpret and translate the seven core ideas I have drawn from physics into usable tools for innovative thinking and improved planning. After your initial read-through of the book, I believe you can use each chapter separately or in combination as ready resources for expanding thought, challenging assumptions, and getting "out of the box."

Each chapter can be used like special-purpose tools by the reader to logically build solid reasons for an idea or argument that might lead to more innovative planning. At the core of any planning process is a sharing of ideas and perspectives. Individual contributions are often a key and can lead to important pivot points. The purpose of this book is to present a list of core ideas that, when reflected upon within the specific context of a particular organization, can inspire *Aha*'s! There is some note-taking space for you at the end of the central chapters.

This book is primarily about the core ideas; however, I wanted to go an extra step and make them usable in real-life planning situations. In this light I have added Chapter 10, which is about personally empowering yourself to use what I am suggesting. I have met a lot of wonderful and smart people in my career and I have seen how who they are as people has made a big difference. The personal energy required to risk suggesting a new or challenging idea is as important as the brilliance to come up with it.

I conclude with some of my own reflections about creativity that emerged as I worked with the ideas during the writing of the book. There will be no "grand theory" in the conclusion that "ties all this together." Not only do I not know one, but as I understand it, the field of physics itself is still searching for one (a giant particle smasher called the Hadron Collider has just been built by the European Organization for Nuclear Research, also known as CERN, at a cost of many billions of dollars to try to figure this out).

As an experienced strategic planner I have included in this book not only ideas and theory, but ways to apply the ideas during a planning process. I use my experience as a consultant and specialist in scenario-based strategic planning to suggest actual techniques for applying what I suggest. You will see this explicitly at the beginning of each chapter, and in particular in the appendix, which addresses the application of my ideas to scenario planning. I hope this material makes this a truly handy little reference book for firing up your plans, opening up paths to innovation, and keeping minds open to more learning.

CHAPTER 1

Learning-Oriented Planning

"We understand that the only competitive advantage the company of the future will have is its managers' ability to learn faster than their competitors."

from Arie P. de Geus, "Planning as Learning"
Harvard Business Review, March–April 1988

AS I WRITE THIS BOOK (the end of 2008 and early months of 2009), the world economy is going through economic turmoil that is being compared to the Great Depression of the 1930s. The economic stress is the result of a host of factors, including bad lending practices in mortgage markets, the creation of complex and hard-to-value financial instruments (known as derivatives), plain old fraud (the Bernard Madoff investment scandal), and, from my point of view, poor strategic planning by the managers of some of the world's biggest companies. Experienced and highly paid executives have mismanaged their companies by not preparing them to deal with changes in the business environment that, in hindsight, seem obvious—in the auto industry rising and volatile oil and gasoline prices, and in the banking sector the truing up of poor credit-based lending practices and the historical fact that housing prices don't always go up. Clearly, whatever strategic plans they had did not work well.

The Need for Better and Innovative Planning

My purpose in writing this book is not to take easy shots at the managers who missed turns in the market and in the process sent their organizations into disaster. I have been an executive working on strategic plans in a large company and have worked with scores of senior executives as a consultant. I understand the macro (economy and industry-wide level), micro (at the company level), and personal (at the level of individuals and relationships) factors that make high-functioning strategic planning and effective follow-through very challenging. My intention here is to address some of the core challenges preventing real breakthrough planning and to offer solutions. Poor and ineffective planning can be replaced with innovative and learning-oriented planning that can help organizations succeed.

My ideas have emerged from my own meditations about a common and recurring problem that I have witnessed over my 20-year career as a strategic planner: groups and managers, while working hard on charting the future of their companies or organizations, settle for ordinary, limited, unimaginative, and, often, dangerous (almost certain to fail) strategies for success. Often a combination of old thinking, attachment to protected or untouchable ideas that are woefully out of date, political maneuvering, and plain fear of an uncertain future cause intelligent and hard-working people to make poor decisions.

I have consistently run into the following three issues as generic blocks to innovative thinking and planning in almost all companies and organizations.

1. Short-term needs (typically for profits or cost savings) tend to drive out the ability to think long-term.

2. The desire and perceived safety of copying competitors precludes real innovation.

3. The perceived safety of protecting sunken investments and their cost advantages means risky new investments are avoided, and the safety of the well-known provides a comfort zone that stifles creativity.

These blocks occur for a good reason; they are the opposite side of grabbing the "low- hanging fruit" of the obvious. But no organization can long survive or reach its full potential by picking only low-hanging fruit. Competition and the inevitable long-term trend of creative destruction (either you or your competitor will bring about evolution in your business) demand that strategic planning be taken seriously. I think this is why, despite those seemingly insurmountable blocks, organizations still take the time to plan. I believe that taking the time is valuable, and that it can be better spent, and can yield more creative and innovative ideas and plans.

To make this true I have embarked on a personal search for something that will help both individuals and groups step outside self-imposed barriers and go for something that will provide specific tools for some really innovative and out-of-the-box thinking. I have found those tools in, of all places, quantum physics.

My purpose in writing this book is not solely to help managers and organizational leaders think differently and see new possibilities. My hope is also that through this kind of new thinking, people will go on to create new kinds of organizations, businesses, and enterprises that will make all of our lives more comfortable, interesting, and prosperous in the future. I believe in a positive future. I believe human beings are at the beginning of a long creative enterprise. I believe scientific discovery and its applications will allow our creativity to outrun our challenges. We need only see the opportunities and be creative in implementing them.

I think with some of the advances we are experiencing (the accelerating pace of nanotech, biotech, information, and communications technologies), we will also need to advance our models of thinking to enable visions of entirely new kinds of organizations, energized to meet human needs and desires that we are just beginning to understand. We will have fantastic new capabilities, and as we make the social, political, and cultural adjustments to these new powers, they will reshape our organizations and thereby our lives.

Just as we have learned from nature's examples on the earth (e.g., triangles and cones to create strong structures or the strength of curly strands of Velcro from the seeds of burdock weeds), I hope this book provides some new tools to enhance and accelerate our ability to think more imaginatively and creatively in building new organizations that use patterns hidden in the subtle structures of the universe.

My Career as a Strategic Planner

In 1978, my first job after graduating from the Graduate School of Business at the University of Chicago was in the international project finance group at Bechtel Corporation (my degrees are in Finance and Economics). After a couple of years there, I joined the Corporate Finance Department of Pacific Gas & Electric Company (PG&E) to work on asset-based financing for power plants and other facilities. In 1986 I was invited to join a select team of managers at PG&E to form its first strategic planning department. We were led by a very intelligent man who had a successful career in strategic planning with some of the leading foundations and organizations involved in thinking about such things as the nuclear weapons complex of the United States. I had previously spent the early part of my career in corporate finance and was thus added to the group for my background in finance and economics. There were several big and interrelated questions facing the company at that time, including

» the beginning of the deregulation-of-markets debacle (which eventually bankrupted PG&E)

» how to deal with changing generation technology (small and renewable power)

» how to move toward a more environmentally friendly business structure

At PG&E I learned the skill of writing long, complex planning documents and managing budgets and programs. During this time I met an interesting group of consultants from a small start-up consulting company, Global Business Network (GBN), who were practitioners of something new to me called "scenario planning." I was asked to lead the company-wide team to apply this technique to augment our strategic planning and help PG&E address the issues outlined above, about which we were highly uncertain. What I found most refreshing about the scenario approach was the open thinking and questioning we were able to do that was far beyond the almost rote approach so common in budget planning ("Ten percent over last year, please!"). As a quick reference, I have included a short introduction to scenario planning in the Resource section on page 130; you can do a Web search and find volumes of information on the subject (including some at www.artofquantumplanning.com).

In 1993, PG&E put in place its first "restructuring." As a key step, the company discontinued operations in the business of engineering and constructing electricity-generating power plants. I was part of a team of four key managers who, over a 45-day period, reassigned about 2000 employees to different parts of the company. The result, unfortunately, was that leading managers of the business unit, including me, were out of a job. However, I had remained in contact with Peter Schwartz, the chairman of GBN, and he invited me to join the company to work with many of their energy and electric-power customers.

I was a part of the GBN consulting practice until 2008 and worked in Asia, Europe, Australia, and all over the United States, not only in the energy industry but also in the fields of mining and metals, telecommunications, information technology, community development, and education. I have applied my skills as a scenario and strategic planner in over 100 engagements. I remain a part of GBN's team of specialists and experts and, when time allows, occasionally participate in scenario work, where my background adds value. Now as president of my own company, I work with companies and nonprofits, assisting them in business and strategic planning. I also love to play the futurist role and speak to organizations about the future of key issues facing them.

This book thus emerges from those 20 years of experience working with CEOs, executive directors, vice presidents, and the teams of people supporting them. Using scenario planning and developed strategies, I and my colleagues at GBN helped to invigorate some new ideas and perspectives and added value to the ongoing strategic conversations and planning processes within the companies and organizations for whom we consulted. But all too often, I left these engagements wondering if we had played it too safe and not pushed harder for more innovative and creative thinking. What additional tools or more thoughtful questions might we have asked? This book is answers that question.

This book also emerges from studying successful and innovative companies and trying to reverse-engineer some of their thinking. Three organizations stand out in my observations: Toyota (and its breakthrough with the Prius), and, in the nonprofit sector, Wikipedia and the

Grameen Bank. These organizations went against so much conventional wisdom (build a car with no proven demand, created an online encyclopedia open to anyone to edit, and, in a respectable manner, lent money to poor people,) that clearly some really innovative thinking had to be in place. From listening to their leaders on various TV programs and in researching their organizations, it is clear that they overcame some tough and entrenched blockages in thinking and creativity. My desire is that the tools in this book will encourage more of that kind of thinking and more of those kinds of solutions and organizations. I hope that by using the seven core ideas for expanding thinking, more people in organizations (and not just the few exceptional visionaries) can create a better future for us all.

Why Quantum Physics?

Finally, here is the story about my route to quantum physics. It started with a movie, then a book, then a furious search on the Web, then more books. The movie was "What the Bleep Do We Know?" Many people (including some of my friends) found this movie irritating and nonsensical. I liked it because it gives hard science a softer and more usable focus for everyday living. I was intrigued that some really great minds were advocating many of its ideas. I then read *The Self-Aware Universe: How Consciousness Creates the Material World*, by Amit Goswami, PhD. At the time I was reading that book, I was leading a significant strategic-planning consulting project in the energy and technology field. As I worked with the client to come up with innovative strategic responses, I was caught again in a frustration loop (how to push the team to think more innovatively while ensuring that core ideas emerged from their minds and not mine).

It was months later that some of the ideas I had researched on quantum physics began to gestate the list of seven ideas included in this book. I read about basic quantum physics in introductory books, I read about Albert Einstein, and I even read science fiction ideas on how physics applies (see my suggestions in the bibliography). There was no flashing blinding light—more like a slow burn with occasional sparks. For a couple of years, what kept me coming back to the quantum physics ideas were regular flashes of new perspectives I got from using them to explain both successes and failures I was seeing in the strategies of organizations (examples are provided in the following chapters). I believe this list of seven ideas from quantum physics, if planted in the minds of people making future plans for their organizations, can provide the sparks for some breakout thinking and more creative and innovative formulation of strategies.

Strategy, Thinking, and Learning-Oriented Planning

I sometimes define strategic planning as the process of making decisions and taking actions that will be impossible or very difficult to reverse. Strategy is the reasoning and rationale behind investing the resources of an organization into the creative process.

Strategy is a key part of the process of turning ideas into action and reality. Strategy involves putting thinking into action. Formulating strategy involves applying thinking to creativity and problem solving— the more creative the thinking, the better the strategy. When I see a wonderful new product or invention, I often shout, "Who thought of this?!" Every human invention started with a thought aimed at meeting a desire or need. Thinking is so important that René Descartes, the French philosopher and mathematician, suggested with his famous statement "I think, therefore I am" that it validated human existence. One of the ways death is defined is that the person is no longer thinking—a person may be breathing but is "brain dead."

I assert that planning is organizational thinking. One of my former colleagues at GBN, Don Michael, insists planning is learning and learning is planning. I agree, and I want to suggest that strategic planning is the process of thinking about what the organization needs to learn; thus learning-oriented strategy. A learning orientation to strategic planning should focus on areas where the organization is strategically uncomfortable (the areas recognized as important to, but are not a strength of, the organization). Just as learning makes us better people and shores up our weaknesses, a strategic plan that has a learning component is a vital way that an organization can become stronger, more creative, and more innovative.

The objective of strategic planning in any organization should be not only to set direction and guide actions and investments, but also to enable an organization to "learn its way forward" and in the process restructure itself. Following on from the quotation by Arie de Gues at the beginning of this chapter, that the only long-term, sustainable advantage is to learn faster than your competitors, I believe that a learning agenda should be a key output of a quality strategic plan (more on this in the Conclusion).

Where I have seen poor, unimaginative planning done, the key factor is the quality of the thinking, and in many cases a lack of a willingness to think deeply or imaginatively. Too often there is a rush for quick, easily explainable answers that validate someone's frame or worldview. In scenario planning work, often I would have to include the expected future that validates the organization's current plans as one of the scenarios in order to retain the support of key people in the organization. At GBN, we called this the "official future" (oddly enough, sometimes managers were not always clear on what it was or willing to admit or defend it). I was often warned that if I, and the team that I was facilitating, did not include the "official future," we would lack credibility (never mind that what is expected almost never occurs). In many cases, I was amazed at what actually was in the expected future (e.g., continued low or moderate oil prices for car companies) and how vociferously they were argued for by some managers.

But this was just the first level of the problem. The second and deeper level is what George Lakoff is pointing to in *Don't Think of An Elephant*—our thinking fits into some frames and structures of which we are often unconscious. Lakoff states,

> *Framing is about getting language that fits your worldview. It is not just language. The ideas are primary—and the language carries those ideas, evokes those ideas."*

These key metaphors, myths, and archetypes govern our thinking the way interstate highway systems govern how we travel across the country. Those key metaphors, myths, and archetypes arise from some very powerful forces, including our contact with nature and our cultures. When we use a particular word, we are speaking a frame of reference into existence. However, we are just pushing the pedal to the metal and have forgotten that the roads were put there by others. We are unconscious in those moments of the fact that these deeply held notions are shaping our thinking and thus shaping our view of the possible.

In business planning situations I have seen warring departments fight over political control and budgets. These conflicts were often voiced by one group saying of the opposition, "They don't get it" or "Their heads are in the sand." Very often there were conflicting views of market developments, technological developments, customer needs, and expected responses. Listening closely, I could hear very different metaphors used to describe the same market or technological developments. These beliefs were often strongly held, and the losing side would in many cases be on the political outs, if not worse (e.g., at risk of losing their jobs). Maybe in the subconscious minds of people they know, even if they don't acknowledge it, their thoughts are vital in creating the future of their organizations. Their conflicts were about the future!

How and what the people who are involved in business and strategic planning think literally creates the futures of their organizations. Thinking is vitally important. Thoughts lead to the creation of things, and those things are the organization. In a world that is changing at a rapid rate and full of uncertainty, it makes sense to me that strategic planning must be about the organization learning its way forward.

The beauty and genius of scenario planning rests in allowing multiple views of the future, legitimizing different world views or market developments, and thus allowing for the development of alternative perceptions and different metaphors. The names of scenario narratives often capture these metaphors and variations in perception. This book is thus about expanding the metaphors and archetypes and, in the process, expanding perception. The metaphors and ideas I have chosen below have the benefit of reflecting some of humankind's best scientific thinking for how the smallest and biggest things in the universe behave. My experience in playing with these ideas is that they open up completely new avenues of thinking and learning and thus creativity and innovation. They have encouraged me to take second and third looks at a phenomenon or event and see something deeper.

How to Use This Book

This book is written for people who are leading and managing the processes for planning the future of their organizations, regardless of the management structure used to do so. My major objective is to share ideas and tools that will lead to better thinking and, therefore, better planning. This book can be especially useful as a preread before entering the planning process, as a way of warming up the imaginative and creative juices. Read it entirely through once. Make any notes you want in the margins or on the pages provided with suggested questions at the end of the chapters; don't worry about your scribbles making sense to anyone but you. Then look broadly for any examples of the quantum structures and thinking manifesting in organizations you see or read about. Look within your industry and outside of it. Take one idea at a time and try it on in a conversation by forming one or more good questions based on it (experiment to experience—play and don't worry when you don't get a question just right). You will know you are getting there when your questions generate in others a pause for deeper consideration and a richer conversation emerges. Don't mention quantum physics when talking to others about your thinking unless you are prepared for a blank stare and to be ignored.

This book can be useful at any point during a planning process when you (or the group of which you are a part) are stuck in tired or worn-out patterns and need to jump-start more radical and creative thinking. It may also be good to pick this book up when you are awash in confidence that your plan is on target and you cannot possibly think of anything that might disrupt it. Use it as a tool to step outside your comfort zone.

This book is designed so that each of the core chapters on the seven ideas can be used separately. While planning, use the ideas in these chapters to encourage innovative thinking from a different perspective. One tool may be more useful in a given situation than another. A quick review and reread of a particular chapter may be just enough to encourage and crystallize some new thinking. Or it may take a combination of chapters. Just do what works best for you.

CHAPTER 2

From Quantum Physics to Quantum Thinking and Planning

"Thoughts are things."

The title of Chapter 1 of *Think and Grow Rich*, by Napoleon Hill

BEFORE INTRODUCING THE SEVEN IDEAS, I want to share a few words about the importance of thoughts and ideas. Expanding on the idea of thoughts being things, observe that the creation of things begins with a thought. Ideas are where human creativity begins.

The Importance of Ideas

New ideas are historically some of the most powerful forces in all of human history. They are the basis from which we create new things that constantly improve human existence. Therefore, thoughts are the basis from which we create our organizations and their futures. As I have stated earlier, planning is inherently a thinking process. In my experience, the core of poor and inadequate strategic planning is a lack of really good thinking and stimulating ideas. In seeking to support more innovative planning, I thought it beneficial to look where fresh and stimulating ideas are already present. I wanted a source for rich ideas that are not flimsy or ungrounded and that can be used in a fairly straightforward way. I think I have found that balance in the ideas I drew from working through the concepts of quantum physics explained below.

A Few Words of Respect About Physics

I have great respect for two great physicists with whom I have worked in my career: Dr. Amory Lovins at the Rocky Mountain Institute and Dr. Art Rosenfeld of the California Energy Commission, two world-renowned energy experts. What I have observed from working with them is that the science can be very complex but when it works well, it seems to take on a marvelous simplicity. In working with these physicists, I have noticed that explaining complex scientific concepts is not always easy. The concept may be explained from multiple angles, and very often important implications are tied up in the description. A lot of hard work is also done in applying the concepts to get to what later appears as ingenious simplicity (even art) in products and services. I want this same kind of result for you, the reader, and for your organizations. I think your pathway to getting there is to take your time with the concepts, cycle through the ideas, and be willing to take a playful attitude as you do. My descriptions of the ideas are as straightforward as I can get them, but throughout the book you may experience subtle expansions where I think they may help. Feel free to develop your own descriptions as you work with the ideas.

In the event you have forgotten a few of the things that we all were taught in high-school science classes and are basic to understanding the ideas presented in this chapter, here are a few reminders:

1. The smallest particle of any element is called an atom.

2. Protons and neutrons make up the nucleus (center) of the atom; electrons circulate around the nucleus.

3. The electrons are circulating around the nucleus so fast that, under the most powerful microscopes, atoms take on the appearance of a very small cloud.

4. Visible light and other forms of radiation such as X-rays move in waves and are, at the smallest particle level, composed of photons. The photons carry electromagnetic energy.

5. Light travels at just over 186,000 miles per second. This is why turning on lights in an enclosed space appears to instantly light up all parts of it. With the naked eye you cannot see one part of a space lit up before another; light is simply moving too fast. Something moving at the speed of light (for example in a circle) appears to be at many places at the same instant to the naked eye.

Seven Ideas from Quantum Physics

There is no magic formula to the seven ideas I define below. They are not vital to any list of ideas in the study of physics. They are simply the ones that, in my research, have had the most direct application to the planning problems I am attempting to solve. They are roughly organized, from my point of view, from the simple to the increasingly complex. Simply put, they work for me and I think they will work for you.

I define quantum planning as applying some of the central insights and ideas of quantum physics (or mechanics) to improve and enhance the quality of thinking and learning in strategic planning processes. The process I am suggesting is to hold these ideas in your mind as long as you can and to try them in an open-minded manner as tools to expand possibilities, options, and choices. Ask "what if" questions based on these ideas when making plans and wrestling with decisions that have a future dimension to them. They can serve as tools to open up the mind.

The insights and ideas I have selected from quantum physics can contribute new perceptions and thereby help create innovative strategic options for any organization that applies them. I explain the ideas in two steps: first, I describe the seven central insights and ideas of quantum physics, and then, I reinterpret them to how they might be applied to strategic planning and learning for businesses and organizations.

Here are the seven ideas.

1. The Particle-Wave Duality   This states simply that light has the properties of both a particle and a wave. It is both and can have properties similar to a grain of sand and an ocean wave. By being both, it displays the properties of both and can be used in applications as one or the other.

2. The Heisenberg Uncertainty Principle   One cannot simultaneously know both the speed and position of an electron. The very process of trying to measure speed exerts an influence that makes measuring position impossible. The very process of determining the position exerts an influence that makes determining the speed impossible. When precisely measuring the position of an electron, only *probabilities* of its speed can be determined. When measuring the speed of an electron, only *probabilities* of its position can be calculated.

3. *Nothing Is Real Until It Is Observed* The probability of where a particle—a photon of light or electron—exists is reduced when we observe it. There is a small probability that at any given moment a particle could be anywhere within its field of motion. But when it is measured or observed, it is real (to the observer) and is there. When a particle is not being observed, it is still somewhere.

4. *The Illusion of Space and Time* Some events in the universe occur faster than the speed of light and are not confined to time in the sense of the past or the future. Related events can occur over large distances simultaneously or at the same instant in time. Some particles appear to travel at speeds faster than the speed of light. Thus, something can come into existence (occupy space) instantaneously, or in no time, by its rate of speed declining, and two related events can come into existence simultaneously.

5. *The "Many Worlds" Idea* A different point of observation will lead to a different position for a light particle or a different probability of its speed. This relates to the dual particle-and-wave nature of light and how observation determines a result. Two simultaneous observations from different points can give different, true, and accurate measurements. Therefore, there can be multiple realities. This is also true when particles are moving faster than the speed of light. A particle that increases or slows its rate of vibration can disappear or appear in an instant and thereby change what is being observed.

6. *The Unified Field Theory* The four fundamental powers of the universe (strong power between quarks, electromagnetic power between charged particles, weak power between electrons, and gravity between all particles) are unified and connected. This theory states that after the "Big Bang" (the very beginning of the universe), there was one unified power from which the four fundamental powers emerged; these are now connected and must be in balance as energy changes. Everything is connected in a unified field and in balance. The totality of all the powers in the field causes all of existence to come into reality at any given moment. There is no way to completely determine the cause of what exists from the past; there is just the instant-to-instant manifestation of the field of all possibility. What "exists" exists only from a perspective or relative position of any observer in the field of all possibilities. Even time is relative.

7. Everything Is Energy   This is not so much quantum physics but is a basic tenet of physics in general and is captured in the famous equation of Albert Einstein: $E = mc^2$ or "energy equals mass times the speed of light squared" (a very big number). Therefore, all mass is simply energy divided by the square of the speed of light. Everything at its deepest level is composed of energy moving through space. There may be some infinitely tiny particle that is made of something besides energy, but, as I understand it, physicists have not found it yet.

If you are confused after reading the seven concepts, congratulations! If you are totally disbelieving of much of it, again congratulations! I will try to provide some relief (or further confusion) by interpreting the ideas in a business or organizational strategic-planning context. The good news is that this is all of the quantum physics I dare try to explain. You, as the reader, will not have to explain any physics to use the ideas in this book. I will give you some useful "handles" in each chapter with which to use the ideas in your planning, and this is all you will need. Your work is to understand and work with how the core ideas in physics can have parallels in your thinking that open up paths to innovation and learning.

The Quantum Physics Ideas Translated for Learning and Planning in Organizations

The words used to express these ideas are mine alone drawn from my reading of the physics literature. I explain the ideas by introducing them in a simple manner. They are further elaborated in the follow-up chapters.

The Particle-Wave Duality

The needs and wants of a customer can be both discrete and continuous. The purpose of an organization is always both specific and many-faceted. An event in the marketplace can have a distinct implication at one point in time and a different implication at another point in time. Any event can be seen as meaning one thing or many things according to the point of view. There can be stage changes that are discontinuous from all known previous stages. A change in the market can appear seemingly out of nowhere but, once there, can be seen as quite sensible and rational.

The Heisenberg Uncertainty Principle

Every important piece of information cannot be entirely knowable. Nothing can be measured exactly. There is no completion proof that everything important has been considered in making any decision. The best that is possible is some sense of the possibility of an event, action, or development (thus the usefulness of scenarios as a tool of planning to guide thinking deeply about uncertainty and assessing risks). Any analysis will just as likely be wrong as right. (Probability analyses are only as good as the limited and incomplete inputs upon which they are based, which is why all forecasting is of limited value.) Even if some analysis gets it "right," it was a good guess and true *for that moment and from that limited perspective.* An analysis done at one point in time and from a particular perspective (there is no neutral perspective) will be wrong later when viewed from another perspective.

Nothing Is Real Until It Is Observed

Intention plus action makes something real. But once the action is taken and something becomes real, attitudes toward it determine what the significance of it is to any given person regardless of the original intention. A company may produce a product or service it expects to be used by consumers in a certain way, only to find out consumers see it differently, and therefore the product or service becomes something else. Further changes by the company to the product or service may be subject similarly unpredictable responses by consumers.

The Illusion of Space and Time

Time itself is a mental construction we human use to coordinate activities and measure the movement of the sun around the earth, and the earth around the sun (in the universe an insignificant planet and an insignificant star). Any idea based on a time sequence is true only for the person perceiving that sequence; it does not exist as a fact in the universe. The idea of a particular "that" which must precede a specific "this" is an illusion in the mind. The history of a business or organization need not constrain its future. The past, and perceptions about the future, are not limiting factors of what is actually possible. Perceptions about the future are one of many points of view and can influence reality only if believed. Believing a different future helps create it. A team of believers might be able to create anything.

The "Many Worlds" Idea

Perceptions about the larger world-view of a market, business environment, industry structure, or set of relationships vary widely. Any perceptions about how a sequence of events might lead to specific conditions are valid only from a particular perspective. At any moment, the business environment can change for seemingly unrelated or related reasons and allow whole new possibilities for creation to open. Locking in on a particular way of seeing, operating, and acting as if that worldview is the only possibility carries risks. Periodically a willingness to fearlessly challenge a world-view from multiple angles, down to core assumptions, beliefs, values, and perceived facts, is a must. The very act of changing perceptions makes those alternative worlds possible and potentially real. A change in perception by a single person with a new observation has the potential to make an alternative world possible.

The Unified Field Theory

In an organization, the view of the business environment (the field) equates to an assessment of how all the factors that influence business conditions relate (including, among others, competitive market conditions, economic conditions, regulatory conditions, and natural or ecological conditions). What a person or group believes about the factors in the business environment shapes what they believe is possible for the organization to create. At any given point there are an infinite number of possibilities for new products and services. However, there is the requirement of balance, which constrains the extremity of conditions in the business environment and what is possible for the organization to create. There must be a balance between strong and weak forces in the business environment that can be brought about over time. There are many ways to characterize them (for example, the economy being strong, and for some, the daily weather perhaps being weak). In conjunction with the infinite creative possibilities for products and services, there are an infinite number of ways that forces may be in balance in the business environment at any given moment. Therefore, being open to a wide range of possibilities is a requirement for creating both products and services and conditions in the business environment under which they may succeed or fail. Within the field, products and services and business conditions are interacting with one another.

Everything is energy, or $E = mc^2$

A business or organization is an energy system designed to meet human needs and desires. E, or the energy of the business or organization, is the attractiveness, integrity, and usefulness of the product or service being produced to meet a need or desire. To the extent it produces something that connects with the need or desire in a powerful way, it has energy. The m, mass, represents hard and soft assets (the physical and human-related assets) organized to produce services or products. The c, or constant, squared is the positive (i.e., multiplicative) relationship between the ideas of driving a business and their connection with the values of the customers served. The easier it is for customers to have their needs and wants met (which they value), the more energy there is in the business or organization. An organization will have more energy when its hard and soft assets are infused with ideas that work together to meet the values of its customers in an efficient manner.

Phew! I hope you got all of that. But don't worry if you didn't. I expand on these ideas in subsequent chapters and give you some ways to use the ideas to create more challenging and creative plans. What is useful at this point is to begin holding the ideas in your mind and collecting possible examples that resonate in your industry or market. If you can, begin to play with some of the concepts to seek explanations for what may be going on in a business situation that is important to you.

In Chapters 3–9 I explain and interpret the seven core ideas. Instead of repeating the physics of the ideas, I concentrate on how you can apply the ideas from physics to planning for businesses and organizations. I follow these explanations with some specific suggestions on how to apply the ideas in actual planning processes. At the ends of Chapters 3–9 I provide space for you to capture your ideas and begin to build on them. I recommend that you first read the chapters in order and then, after you have become familiar with them, that you refer to specific chapters to get insights into particular situations. Play with the chapters as tools to deepen your understanding of the patterns you see, and don't be afraid to "mix and match" if that works for you.

CHAPTER 3

Thinking
Beyond Duality

I CHOSE THE TITLE OF THIS CHAPTER CAREFULLY, because the key idea here points directly to how one thinks. What I mean by dual thinking here is not the obviously wrong approach to thinking that says, "Since it is not this, it must be its opposite." My point here is not to warn people about on-the-surface or oversimplified thinking; in other words, I am not warning against plain lightweight thinking. What I am aiming at here is the slippery process of positionality—taking a position, holding to it, and arguing from it as if it were the absolute truth.

Getting Out of the Duality Trap

The process of taking a position and defending it leads to polarization and therefore narrow thinking. When I have witnessed really poor planning, often I have observed that it was due to someone's holding a position and, given their power in the organization, dominating the thinking, planning, and, more importantly, the creative and imagina-

Chapter Overview

Idea from Physics
Light has the properties of both a particle and a wave. It is both.

Idea Translated for Planning
Avoid the trap of dualistic thinking and either/or types of analyses. Any analysis based on either/or thinking is simplistic and false. Analyses of opportunities, risks, major trends, and big issues must extend beyond a "good or bad" type of thinking. Innovation will be revealed by questions that extend beyond duality and encourage learning and "both/and" thinking.

Applications for Planning

» Identify dualistic thinking in the analysis that supports assessments of key factors and trends, and important decisions.

» Break up dualistic thought patterns when they occur by thinking in patterns that are "around, inside and outside, and over and under" the issue being addressed.

» Find extra time to look at the broader context around important decisions to identify currently insignificant factors that have potential to become critical.

» Capture any new insights from the steps above and integrate them into the original analysis or decision.

tion processes of a group. People who do this are not consciously or intentionally trying to kill creativity. Often they think they are doing the group a favor, saving some time, getting people on the right track. They are not conscious of the trap of dual thinking that they have set up. The polarity they cause kills creativity and innovation with the oversimplification of duality.

Duality-Based Thinking

The following quote from Dr. David Hawkins, *The Eye of the I, from Which Nothing Is Hidden,* captures a lot for me.

> *Arbitrary selectivity results in a positionality, which is a point of view that artificially polarizes the oneness of Reality into seemingly separate parts. These parts are apparent only, and not actually separate in Reality. The separation into parts occurs only in the mind and not in Reality. Thus we end up speaking of 'here' and 'there' or 'now' versus 'then,' or we arbitrarily select out portions from the flow of life that we refer to as 'events' or 'happenings.' One serious consequence of this mental process is the production of a false understanding of causality. This misunderstanding leads to endless human problems and tragedies.*

This quote from Dr. Hawkins is a capsule definition of what I see as the trap of dualistic thinking. He is pointing out that our thoughts and ideas, which are so obvious and valuable to us, are actually quite arbitrary. If I assert that Bill Clinton was a great president, it is quite an arbitrary statement, regardless of how much I believe it to be true. It is totally dependent on my point of view, my values, my educational background, my political values, my view of history, and on and on. The statement that Bill Clinton was a great President is simply not universally true.

Even if we think we know what we are talking about, we must understand that we don't actually *know* what we are talking about in terms of a direct, replicable experience that is not in some way entirely subjective. Going back to my assertion about Bill Clinton, when I try to put a real sense of knowing around this, it gets foggy. Exactly what experience makes me think this? Is it that I simply like his personality, or that I feel he was mistreated by people I didn't like, or I had a good job during his tenure—exactly what is it? Where dangerous duality slips in is when I take a position on Bill Clinton and then argue against anyone who has a contrary view, when I see anyone who disagrees with me as out of touch or stupid or evil. J. Krishnamurti has a great explanation of what is going on at a deep level in such a process in his book, *Freedom from the Known.* He says:

> *I lead a certain kind of life; I think in a certain pattern; I have certain beliefs and dogmas and I don't want those patterns of existence disturbed because I have my roots in them. I don't want them to be disturbed because the disturbance produces a state of unknowing and I dislike that. If I am torn away from everything I know and I believe, I want to be reasonably certain of the state of the things to which I am going. So the brain cells have created a pattern and those brain cells refuse to create another pattern which may be uncertain. The movement from certainty to uncertainty is what I call fear.*

Instances of false dual thinking that I have encountered in organizations are generally based on arguments with the following characteristics.

1. They are tied to a past experience that the person (especially a powerful leader) sees as formative.

2. They are associated with a person of power or prestige in the organization who is not lightly challenged.

3. They are protective of some idea or belief viewed as special or sacred in the organization, even though it is being held way beyond its usefulness.

4. The presumed cost of thinking differently is prohibitive (thus the opportunity cost of thinking differently or the catastrophic cost of holding onto something that might be crushed by much

more powerful forces in the market or business environment is not taken into account).

Whichever of these is the case, the net impact is a slide down the slippery slope of the trap of dualistic thinking.

An example of getting out of the duality trap and finding success in a big company, in my view, is the strategy the Proctor & Gamble Company introduced in 2008 in its *Pūr* water purification business. *Pūr* is a brand of filters and bottles that allows consumers to filter out impurities in tap water. As many people have become concerned about what's in their water, they have sought out options like *Pūr*, as well as bottled water. Proctor & Gamble also sells *Pūr Flavor Options,* which actually puts something *back* into the water the customer just purified. This turns around the whole point of pure water. *Pūr Flavor Options* are basically fruit-flavored concentrates with a little artificial sweetener. So a water purification business is now allowing consumers to not drink pure water! I can only imagine how this idea might have gone over when initially suggested. The product has proved to be very popular with young people.

As I mentioned earlier, the needs and wants of a customer can be both discrete and continuous. The purpose of an organization is always both specific and many-faceted. An event in the marketplace can have a distinct implication at one point in time and a different one at another point in time. Any event can be seen as meaning one thing or many things, according to the point of view. There can be state changes that are discontinuous from all known previous states. A change in the market can appear seemingly out of nowhere, but once there it can be seen as quite sensible and rational. Pushing these kinds of ideas in the middle of a planning process with a team of super-smart managers who are one side of a dualistic thought process leads to a kind of shunning—despite the need for some new and creative thinking. What drives this kind of behavior? In my experience, the following:

1. The desire to speed up work as an indicator of efficiency.

2. The misplaced notion that just because thoughts are logical, they have a large chance of being true.

3. The minimizing or discounting of the change, and the changeable nature of the assumptions upon which an argument is based.

These three can combine and yield a powerful force that shuts down thinking and pushes a group quickly onto one side of a dualistic thought process. It leads to a premature consensus. This consensus then gives a false sense of safety that locks the door on any further thought or creativity.

A tragic example of this at the end of 2008 contributed to the failure of the Lehman Brothers investment bank. It was widely reported that Lehman's powerful chairman was convinced the problems of the company were mostly due to short-sellers and a need for more capital. The fact that global credit markets had entered a historical freezing up, causing a radical shift in assessing risk, was recognized far too late to save the company. Lehman's competitors at Merrill Lynch, with a relatively new chairman, moved fast at the same time to sell their company to Bank of America and begin to restructure the company to deal with the new realities.

Escaping the Duality Trap in Planning

The first step to getting beyond dualistic thinking is to recognize it—in particular to recognize it at pivotal decision points. Turning the knowledge into a real change in behavior demands some practice. For many people (including me) it may take practice to recognize it not only with the mind but with feelings as well. In the process of listening for it, you may need to develop over time an inner radar that goes off when you hear someone holding tightly to a position. In my experience, the question arises, "Does it *have* to be this way?" The "it" in the previous sentence may be their way of thinking, my way of thinking, or that particular position.

Recognizing dualistic thinking in one's own thinking is clearly the best place to start. Question your own assumptions and ask deeply if you really *know* what you are saying or thinking. Is it just an opinion? Back to Hawkins, who says:

> We tend to cling to thoughts because the ego, in its vanity, classifies them as 'mine.' This is the vanity of possession which automatically adds value and importance to anything (possessions, country, relatives, and opinions) as soon as the thought 'mine' is prefixed. Once the supposed value of a thought has been enhanced by the prefix 'mine,' it now takes on a tyrannical role and tends to dominate thought patterns and automatically distorts them.

Having personal ownership of an idea as "mine" automatically leads to taking a position, which then immediately violates the particle-wave duality principle. Taking a position is saying that light is only a particle or that an idea is discrete and does not change as it evolves. Doing so has the effect of slicing the world into two, even though it is much more than this. The intentional or unconscious creating of opposition and a potential for conflict by taking a position kills the opportunity for deeper thinking and creativity.

I have found it useful to find examples in my business experience of destructive positional thinking and to ponder them. An example that was instructive for me during my career in the electric power industry in the 1990s was the position that competition would be good for the industry and result in lower prices. This position was widely argued and held by energy economists and CEOs throughout the industry. Changes in regulations in many states were put in place to implement this idea. Applying this idea to the industry eventually led to one of the biggest debacles in business history and billions of dollars in losses.

California, which was a state on the leading edge of the move toward competition in this sector, saw a run-up in prices and bankruptcies in the power sector of the state. However, during the early stages of the rise of this idea of competition (and in some minds still to this day), arguments to the contrary were viewed as backward and out of date. The core of why this idea of competition proved so wrong was that it was based on an assumption that electric power was a product sold to a customer in a market. Over time it became clear that electricity was a necessity delivered to a citizen through investment by private industry with government oversight. Taking this view (which was a traditional view held by companies that stayed out of the fray) would have called into question the free-market positionality that led to a debacle. As California and other states plowed ahead, several states and their power companies watched from the sidelines and, by holding back, avoided billions of dollars in losses and high prices.

I urge you to look into your industry or area of work to find examples of dualistic thinking that blinds insight and short-circuits thinking. Examples that pinpoint costs may resonate strongly with your colleagues. Positive examples of when dualistic thinking was avoided and led to a success can also be helpful. Compiling a list of examples will be a good thought exercise to help you absorb the ideas in this chapter.

An end-of-chapter worksheet has been provided for your use in taking notes relevant to the ideas in Chapter's 3–9. If you have purchased this book, please use the worksheets provided. If you have borrowed the book from a library, please copy the worksheets or prepare your own.

Personal notes and ideas

Examples for my industry

Examples from other industries

Potential good questions

4

Inescapable Uncertainty

TWO ESSENTIAL POINTS EMERGE from the Heisenberg Uncertainty Principle of quantum physics: You can't simultaneously know the position and direction of something (for example, in physics, a light particle); and attempt to find out one or the other influences of the very thing you are trying to figure out. Thus, there is a limit to what we can know precisely, and there is no unbiased point of view from which to know anything.

Embracing Uncertainty

In *The Self-Aware Universe: How Consciousness Creates the Material World,* Amit Goswami, Richard E. Reed, and Maggie Goswami express this point in an interesting manner by saying the following.

> *You may ask, is there any evidence at all that the ideas of quantum mechanics apply to the brain-mind? There seems to be at least circumstantial evidence. David Bohm and before him August Conte noted that there seems to be an uncertainty*

Chapter Overview

Idea from Physics

It is impossible to simultaneously know both the position and the speed of an electron. The process of measuring one exerts influences that make it impossible to accurately measure the other.

Idea Translated for Planning

There is no way to escape uncertainty in the business environment or marketplace. A good analysis can never be a complete analysis. Any "right" answer is "right" only in a limited context. Therefore, all analyses must be used in a learning-oriented mode. Questions about assumptions and context should be vigorously pursued to support more open learning.

Applications for Planning

» The planning process must be understood as, and structured to be, a learning-oriented process. A learning loop must be embedded in which new information is captured and processed in the ongoing planning process.

» Leaders must strongly support a learning environment where good questions are encouraged and appreciated.

» Regular use of scenario analysis will support an understanding of the changing context of the business environment and create a learning-forward agenda.

» Connect the results of the learning-forward agenda to innovation and to building adaptability into the organization.

principle operating for thought. If we concentrate on the content of thought, we lose sight of the direction in which thought is heading. If we concentrate on the direction of thought, we lose sharpness in its content. Observe your thoughts and see for yourself.

The Goswamis and Reed point out that concentrating on something with the mind, inherently introduces the chance of a misperception: while thinking about the specifics of an idea, we lose sight of the trend in which it might evolve. In conversation, there is a parallel in trying to understand simultaneously exactly what someone is saying and that person's underlying meaning: the mind literally has to separate the two to get an approximation of true understanding. We hear the words and then reflect on the deeper meanings.

Inescapable Uncertainty Based on Position and Direction

The position/direction problem should be the final nail in the coffin of duality-based thinking. By holding a firm position on how you perceive something, you can't accurately predict how it might change. And if you are sure about how something is trending or evolving, it is very hard to predict its state at a given point in the future. There is no choice but to embrace uncertainty as a natural state.

I have tried the Bohm/Conte thought experiment suggested by Goswami, and it is dead-on. I have even used it to determine the nature of a disagreement. In many cases there is an unrealized confusion about whether a conversation concerns the specific state of an issue at the moment or the direction it may be moving toward. As an example, when my wife and I are struggling to manage our budget, I often place an emphasis on exactly what is in the account currently while she may be more focused on how much may be coming in over the next couple of weeks.

Taking the time to understand the meaning being attached to important ideas by separating the specifics from the direction of change can be very powerful in a planning process. I think this has been an unconscious motivation for many companies to do scenario work on technologies and technological change. Consider the evolution of the cell phone. Early cell or mobile phones were just that, phones that were movable. Nowadays a cell phone is a phone, camera, Internet device, global positioning system (GPS) navigator, notebook, calendar, and music player; it has become more widely known as a personal digital assistant (PDA) thatn as a cell phone. By 2010, it may become a medical device or even something else.

The position versus direction-of-change issue can also be used to understand the rationales behind strategic decisions. What aspects of the decision are hinging on position versus direction? A company may decide to enter a new market because of profits they see in the market today without recognizing the trajectory of those profits (especially as would be feasible after they enter the field and open the door for more competition and pressure on prices). When the direction-of-change aspect is missed, it can lead to organizations prematurely entering markets for which they have no real long-term commitment or the willingness to do the continuous learning that might be involved in longer-term success.

Again, the point here is to open up one's thinking by truly understanding that not knowing can actually be a good thing. Not knowing doesn't mean that one is unintelligent; it means that there is an open space upon which to build a continuously developing understanding. A premium is now given to curiosity, learning, experimentation, and reflection.

In dealing with the direction-of-change aspect and succeeding, despite inescapable uncertainty, I can think of no better an organization than The Learning Annex. Founded in 1980, it was sold in 1991

and repurchased in 2002 by Bill Zanker, its founder. A bright entrepreneurial couple, Stephen Seligman and Beth Greer, bought it for a
few hundred thousand dollars in 1991 and sold it back to Zanker
for millions in 2002. The Learning Annex became the largest private
alternative-adult education company in the U.S., helping thousands
of people see new possibilities and feel empowered to make changes
in their lives. Learning Annex instructors, experts in their fields and
frequently best-selling authors, make money on the class fees and on
books, CDs, or other material they can sell in the back of the room.
During the eleven years Stephen Seligman and Beth Greer owned the
company, they poured in hours of hard work, but they realized something very important in the beginning: they could not know in advance
what their customers would be interested in learning more about! There
was no certainty that people were interested in learning belly dancing
rather than dream interpretation, or opening a coffee house rather than
a T-shirt company. So they ran their business with a few rules.

1. Don't assume what the customer wants.

2. Give a presenter a chance to sell to customers without losing
    money.

3. Present the information to the customer in a short (three hours
    or less), easy-to-understand manner.

4. Hold the classes at convenient locations.

Beth used herself as the role model for her target market. When
she owned the business, she was the typical Learning Annex student:
between 30 and 45 years old, with no young children or grown children, and an interest in personal improvement. She ran classes that
she herself would enjoy, and nine times out of ten they were successful. Over time, Stephen and Beth got a better sense of what kinds of
classes were popular, but they never got to the point of narrowing their

offerings. They always had the "oddball" class like "How to Start a Goat Farm," which turned out to be a huge success. They also became very good at coaching and giving potential presenters a good idea of how to succeed. Their approach to managing inescapable uncertainty was to "learn through doing and through meeting people." Over time, as they expanded the company into major cities and got it well known from catalogs placed in street boxes, they created brand identity. The Learning Annex became so well known that it was even parodied on *The Simpsons* and *Saturday Night Live,* and appeared on popular TV programs such as *Sex and the City* and *The Tonight Show with Jay Leno.* As the adult-education, conferencing, and public-speaking business took off in the early 2000s, Beth and Stephen sold it back to Bill Zanker, at a healthy profit. Bill and his group poured in more capital and went after bigger names (e.g., Donald Trump) and grew the business even further.

Inescapable Uncertainty Based on Connection Between Actions and Context

The idea that what I do, say, or think affects what I perceive to exist and might impact what actually exists is a brain-twisting thought. How I look at something (my attitude toward it) affects what I see (how I define it) and what it may become. If I change how I look at something (my attitude toward it), then it can become something totally different now and possibly in the future.

As someone with a background in economics, I find the way George Soros talks about the interconnections between actions and context in *The Alchemy of Finance* especially enlightening. He says:

> The generally accepted view is that markets are always right—that is, market prices tend to discount future developments accurately even when it is unclear what those developments are. I start with the opposite point of view: I believe that market prices are

always wrong in the sense that they present a biased view of the future. But distortion works in both directions: not only do market participants operate with bias, but their bias can also influence the course of events. This may create the impression that markets anticipate future development accurately, but in fact it is not present expectations that correspond to future events, but future events that are shaped by present expectations. The participants' perceptions are inherently flawed, and there is a two-way connection between flawed perceptions and the actual course of events, which results in a lack of correspondence between the two. I call this two-way connection "reflexivity."

What Soros points out in his special way is that our expectations today influence the shape of the future we are planning for (in quantum physics, "observing influences what you are observing").

One easy way I have found to ground my understanding of this highly variable connection between actions and context is in thinking about my relationship with my son. He is a college student and, at age 21, faces a lot of uncertainty in his life: In what area does he want to concentrate his studies? What girls should he date? How should he spend his summer earnings? Should he participate in sports while in college? The list goes on. What I have found is that my attitude toward those decisions impacts how he makes them in ways that I surely cannot predict. How I think he might react to what I say impacts how I say it. So if I say I like a certain girl he is dating, is this good for her or not? Should I say nothing at all if I like her so that I don't make him feel that I am pressuring him to like her more than he actually might? My ability to influence the selection of my future daughter-in-law is full of uncertainty and two-way connections. How might the young lady's perception of me impact my son's perception of her? Now the context has shifted to her perspective! If she overhears me making a positive comment about her to my son, how might her view of his reaction affect the relationship? Whatever prediction I might make of their future relationship therefore has a very high probability of being wrong, and my actions may in the end have contributed to an undesired result.

To make this coincept more applicable to businesses, what happens when a company makes a new product or service announcement? The announcement itself has changed the dynamics of the market that the product is about to enter because all of the direct competitors will then begin to make adjustments to their products and services. Prices and features may change on competitive products and services overnight. It is this additional level of thinking that I often see missed or cut short in planning sessions. The rush factor can play a big role.

Inescapable Uncertainty in the Planning Process and Learning

Very often in planning sessions the question comes up, "What might we be missing?" The response is normally dead silence. Or a few brave souls may suggest a few ideas, but seldom with any context. Here is a set of questions connected to the inescapable uncertainties that might provide that context.

1. Have we separated the specifics of our idea(s) from where it (they) may be evolving?

2. If we are focusing on a trend, do we know enough about how the trend may manifest at a particular point?

3. How might our actions impact the context and environment in which we are taking them, what interactions do we expect, and what are our plans to meet those interactions?

The point of these questions (and others you may think of) is to embrace uncertainty and use it to direct learning and exploration. This is also the point where learning and using imagination can connect. Uncertainty is thus pointing the way to what the organization needs to learn! Unfortunately, in the haste to "do something," taking time to generate questions is often seen as a waste of time in planning. Sometimes that "something" that needs to be done is learning and sharing.

What makes inescapable uncertainty easier to deal with in a planning process is to resist the need for a false sense of closure. Certainly, the planning process and selection of strategies should come to an end so that actions can be taken. But when those moves are made, there should be a sense that there are still things that are unclear and uncertain and that the learning process remains open. Planning can even proceed with a sense of confidence, but care should be taken not to move from confidence to hubris. The integration of a learning agenda in the ongoing planning process is needed so that the strategic conversation remains open. Periodic updates on the answers and insights gained from working on key questions are a key part of what I have witnessed in the most effective strategic planning processes.

Chapter 5 may also give some comfort because there is some power in having an intention.

Personal notes and ideas

Examples for my industry

Examples from other industries

Potential good questions

5

Intentions, Actions, and Reality

THE PROBABILITY OF WHERE A PARTICLE is actually located is reduced when you observe it. This law of quantum physics about observation collapsing probability into reality truly amazed me. The idea that the very fact of observing something is related to its being there was a shock! It is not that something doesn't exist when you are not observing it (your car is still in the driveway even though you are not looking at it), but even on the very tiny scale of the universe there is a large range of probabilities.

The Power and Limits of Intention in an Organization

One way to see what I mean by "collapsing" is to stand directly in front of a large mirror and and note what you see. Then move sharply to the right or left and see how the reflection changes. Those things you saw on the right still exist on the right, but your change in position has thus led to the reflection's "collapsing" into your new frame of reference.

Chapter Overview

Idea from Physics

The probability of where a particle actually is gets reduced when it is observed. Measurements are real only at the point from which they are observed. Observations influence what is measured at the point and the time of the observation.

Idea Translated for Planning

Intentions, and the perceptions that support them, are powerful and meaningful. The intentions of the organization give focus to and influence events in the business environment. However, those intentions cannot totally determine conditions in the business environment. The perceptions of the organization about the meaning of events or trends are valid only from the organization's viewpoint. Alternative viewpoints should be aggressively pursued as tools for learning.

Applications for Planning

» Set clear intentions for the organization and be explicit in revealing the core beliefs and perceptions that support them.

» Openly share intentions and perceptions, and regularly seek the views of others (outsiders) about them. Process any new insights, especially those that conflict with the core beliefs and ideas of the organization, in a learning-oriented mode.

» Regularly check important intentions against changing conditions in the business environment by embedding a learning process around them. Combine both expert interviews and scenario analysis as appropriate to the resources of the organization.

Another way of stating this collapsing principle is that our intentions set our perceptions and thus make what we perceive into reality. Having an intention colors the water, filters out some colors, and sets the frame of reference. Here is a short story that I heard that captures this concept. This story is paraphrased from one heard on National Public Radio, October 2008.

A Dead Rat Story

Women are generally afraid of, or at least averse to, dead rats. A young man who lived in San Francisco was called by a single mother, who was a friend of his, to remove a dead rat from her garage. He was called to this noble duty because he was the only person she knew who was known to enjoy hunting. Since hunting involves killing animals, she figured he was just the person for the job. When he arrived, the young daughter of his friend, who was about 5 years old, greeted him at the door and anxiously took him to the deceased rodent. Her young face was full of wonderment as well as fear. At this moment, he had a flash of insight—this was a teachable moment. As the young girl watched over his shoulder and as he lifted the rat with a shovel into a plastic bag, he decided to explain some of what she was observing. First, he explained that the ants that had covered the rat were showing how nature recycles. Second, he explained germs and why it was important not to touch the dead rat. And finally, he described a little bit of anatomy and how rats could flatten their bodies and squeeze into small places. This is how a dead rat became a lesson that science teachers could appreciate.

The point I draw from the *Dead Rat Story* is that how you perceive something, and how open you are to an experience, can make a big difference in what it is—a dead rat can be a science project! An intention only to see the worst aspects of a dead rat make it just that. What this says for organizations and planning is that how we define things and describe things from our point of view determines what they are. But avoid an unhealthy positionality: what can be forgotten is the probability part. Before you define something as "that," it can be many other things. What's more, as soon as you stop being the point of reference from which something is being defined, it can be something else. Different persons with different intentions can create different realities from the exact same circumstances.

An example of this is playing out within about a mile of my home. In the last year, both a Whole Foods Market and a Trader Joe's have opened near my home in Oakland, California, near an area called Lake Merritt. The stores are very different physically. The Whole Foods Market is a large architectural masterpiece built in what was an abandoned Cadillac dealership. The Trader Joe's is a smaller, funkier place built in the middle of a busy shopping district.

Both of these companies are clearly aiming at people who want more organic foods, good wines, fresh vegetables, and slightly exotic or gourmet foods, and who want the company they buy from to evidence some concern about healthy lifestyles and the environment. They both see a shift in consumer preferences toward more healthful eating but are taking different approaches to profiting from it. In many cities in the U.S., both companies have expanded greatly in the last decade and taken lots of market share from traditional grocers like Safeway Foods. Trader Joe's is privately held and Whole Foods is publicly traded. Both have been very successful. Whole Foods stores tend to be bigger and offer a more complete line of items. Despite some recent changes, it is not seen as a low-cost food store, but as one that offers high quality for a price. Whole Foods Stores are big enough to encourage a lot more roaming and incidental purchases. Trader Joe's markets are generally smaller and offer a much more limited range of products such as soaps and other personal items; generally they do not offer items such as plastics. On some items, Trader Joe's is very cost-competitive, but it really is not a low-cost food store. With its smaller stores, location seems to be a big part of their competitive strategy as well. I also find more prewrapped items in Trader Joe's than in Whole Foods and it seems to be targeted at "convenience." Both stores have been so successful that they are putting pressure on traditional middle-market grocers like Safeway to change. They are causing a shift in the food market leading to an identified low and bulk end, dominated by companies like Costco and Walmart, a very thin middle market (Safeway), and Whole Foods and Trader Joe's dominating the high end.

A look at the history of these two high-end companies provides a partial explanation of their different approaches. Trader Joe's was started by Joe Coulombe and originated with a small chain of stores in the Los Angeles area called Pronto Market. Coulombe's goal was to compete with 7-Eleven stores, and he was having a hard time of it. So deep in the origins of Trader Joe's is a convenience-store concept. On the other hand, Whole Foods has its origin with its founders John Mackey and Rene Lawson, whose original store was called Safer Way Natural Foods. Within two years of founding their original store, they hooked up with two other people, Craig Weller and Mark Skiles, who had founded Clarksville Natural Grocery. That original store was 12,500 square feet and had a staff of 19 people. It is clear that in the "DNA" of Whole Foods was a larger, almost full-service approach. Two different founding approaches led to different approaches at serving the growing market for organic and health-oriented eating and living. The teams saw the world differently from their different perspectives.

At the time of the writing of this book (the end of 2008 and beginning of 2009), there is, in my view, no more amazing and tragic example of how dangerous a stuck intention and positionality can be than the contribution to the credit crisis made by the Federal Reserve Bank of the United States over the previous decade. Note this admission from Alan Greenspan, the Chairman of the Federal Reserve, in his testimony before the House Committee on Oversight and Government Reform as quoted on October 28, 2008 in the *New York Times*:

> *Those of us who have looked to the self-interest of lending institutions to protect shareholder equity, myself included, are in a state of shocked disbelief.*

I too learned the free-market gospel during my education at the University of Chicago, and so, during the last decade, I also leaned toward the ideas held by Dr. Greenspan; I am not holding him up to ridicule here. The point is that intention and positionality indeed do not cause reality. What they actually cause is a closed mind and an inability to see real changes in the real world.

It is now easier to see why keeping an open mind is such a challenge—because when you make an observation in your mind, whatever you are observing collapses into being what you think it is. Your observation has made it real in your eyes and mind, and it becomes "yours." For that moment you cannot see it any other way; until your perspective changes, something literally *is* what's in your mind. You have collapsed the probabilities of what it might be to what it is. Your decision to collapse something into what it is derives from your previous experiences and acquired knowledge. You have a basis for saying what something is that has roots in your experience. Being open, therefore, may not only come up against the pressure of your instant assessment and seeing something as it *is* in that moment, but it may also require that you overturn years of history and experience—a very tall order! It is painful to be open to an alternative point of view because it goes against everything you think you see and everything you have ever thought you saw and experienced in the past! Unfortunately, all of this still does not make your decision about something the *only* thing it can be.

There are thus two distinct points to hold in your mind in using the process of observation collapsing probability into reality. First, the "collapse to reality" definition exists only for the person taking that point of view at a given moment. Whatever is being observed is real for that person at that time from his or her perspective only. It is not the same for another person looking at the same thing from a different point of view or at a different point in time. Second, the collapse into reality is only one of many possible realities, and there is value (something new may be seen) in reobserving. What quantum physics tells us is that the very nature of the universe suggests that you constantly check your perceptions; no matter how "right" you think you are, there is a built-in probability that you are wrong. There is something better than being right; it is being open to constant learning to allow readjustments to a changing environment. I believe learning leads to flexibility, which in turn opens the door for creativity and innovation. Leaders who deeply understand their need for constant openness to learning will be the ones who can lead their organizations to more innovative and creative development. Imagine, returning to my points about the Federal Reserve's lack of action over the last decade, if changes to policy had been made earlier.

A strong intention can be powerful and energizing; you can't accomplish much without a clear intention. I am in the camp of positive-thinking people who believe in the power of focused intentions—however, not to the point of blindness or willful ignorance. Intention is a powerful influence on helping us create the reality and futures we want, but it alone does not *cause* reality to be incapable of any other alternative. The reality influenced by your intention is also just your point of view of it. A shift in your point of view can open up new and potentially more valuable possibilities. Very often, this shift is needed not only to keep from "going off the rails," but to see an even higher possibility than the one trapped in an old intention.

A story that illustrates the advantages of a shift in perspective is my experience as a baseball fan. I grew up in Chicago as a long-suffering Cubs fan. I remember watching Cub games in which very often the score was 2 to 1, Cubs losing, of course. I am sure these were very well-pitched games, but during my teenage years they were quite boring. I would wait for Ernie Banks to come up, hoping for a home run and some excitement. The batter and getting a hit were the focus of the game for me. During my mid-twenties I moved to the San Francisco Bay Area and became both an Oakland A's and a San Francisco Giants fan. On the Oakland A's team at the time was a wonderful player named Ricky Henderson. Ricky went on to set the record for most stolen bases in American baseball history. He was a good hitter, but his game really came into being once he was on base. His ability to steal a base, and the pressure this put on the pitcher and the opposing team, literally changed the game for me. The pitcher would have to adjust his pitches according to what Ricky was doing. Should he pitch out so that Ricky might be thrown out while attempting to steal? Ricky's activity changed the pitches that the batter would get. The defensive alignment on the field would shift. The opposing manager would get very nervous. The point of watching the game for me became watching Ricky and all the adjustments made to stop *him,* not the batter. Even a game with a final score of 2 to 1 could have been an exciting game because Ricky might have stolen third base in the ninth inning! My whole perspective on the game of baseball shifted.

A wonderful movie that illustrates this point of shifting perspectives and meaning-making is *The Gods Must Be Crazy,* written and directed by Jamie Uys and released in 1980. It tells the story of an African tribesman who finds a Coca-Cola bottle discarded by a European visitor from an airplane flying overhead. Having had no contact with the modern world, the tribesman and his neighbors proceed to do all manner of things with the bottle to make it useful in their culture. At no point do they actually drink out of it.

Observation Collapsing Probability and Planning

In the business arena, Apple provides an illustration of the openness and flexibility required in a world of collapsing probability. Within a few months of the release of the Apple iPhone in 2007, hackers had created new programs that allowed the machine to do a much wider range of things than Apple had intended in its original release. Apple had an agreement with AT&T as the sole telecommunications service provider, and hackers were even able to circumvent the agreement. So much creativity was happening around the device that Apple eventually made a shift to allow some hackers the privilege of being approved by the company. Apple learned from this episode and added some of the features in its next version of the iPhone introduced in 2008.

What this illustrates is that excellent strategic planning demands a constant openness to change based on learning. This is what planning is essentially all about. My GBN colleague, Arie de Geus, has argued that learning faster than your competitors can lead to a competitive advantage (see his *Harvard Business Review* article "Planning as Learning"). I would add that the ability to change faster than your competitors is a competitive advantage. What is learned has to be translated into change.

What this quantum law of observation and collapsing probability suggests strongly for planning is holding a space for a continuous feedback loop of perceiving and change. It works like this:

1. Make initial observations and allow characterization/definition.

2. From the definition, set an intention.

3. Take action based on the intention, but don't take a defensive position.

4. Observe again and discount history and the original definition.

5. Be ready to exchange the original intention for a new one.

6. Repeat steps 1–5 continuously.

This observation of collapsing probability also suggests the usefulness of a large dose of personal humility. Often this is sorely lacking in individuals, and it harms the ability of a group to work and plan together. Creativity and the spirit of the group can thus be crushed. Enthusiasm, which can be a powerful element in completing hard tasks, can be impossible to sustain without humility in the face of what truly is a complex world. In Chapter 10 I will pursue the personal side of good planning more extensively.

Chapter 6 takes a closer look at how organizations perceive time in planning. Get ready to have some openness about "when" things occur.

Personal notes and ideas

Examples for my industry

Examples from other industries

Potential good questions

6

The Illusion of Time and Space (Things and Order)

THE OFTEN-ASKED QUESTION OF WHICH CAME FIRST, the chicken or the egg, captures the deeply held sense there must be some order to things—that there must be a "this" before there is a "that." It is the kind of simple mind trick that nature moved beyond long ago. Whatever the answer is, it did not constrain the power of nature to make both the chicken and the egg.

Avoiding the Trap of Sequential Thinking and the Illusion of Logic

"This" coming before "that" is somehow not a constraint on creativity. This is a core idea planners must hold as they help their organizations move into the future. "This" before "that" is an illusion that exists only in the mind of the thinker; it is not reality. The sequence is the thinker's alone and not backed up by the universe. No matter how beautiful a

Chapter Overview

Idea from Physics

Some events in the universe occur at speeds faster than the speed of light and are not confined to time in the sense of the past or the future. Some particles appear to travel at speeds beyond the speed of light and can be in multiple places at the same instant.

Idea Translated for Planning

Over time, any analysis or ideas based on a particular sequence of events cannot be proven to be true. At most, these ideas are perceptions based on particular assumptions, observations, and points of view. Change assumptions, add new observations, and shift the point of view, and another plausible sequence is possible. Making those changes and keeping an open attitude toward them must be the core of learning-oriented strategic planning.

Applications for Planning

» Challenge and change assumptions to vary the time sequence in an analysis supporting an important decision or idea.

» Seek new observations or ideas that might change the time sequence in an analysis.

» Capture what is learned from the previous steps for sources of creativity or innovation.

» Note well any strategic decisions based on time-sequenced arguments, and build adaptability into those decisions from what is learned from the previous steps.

sequentially logical argument is, it is not true for all time, all people, and all situations.

That there must be an order of things arranged at a fundamental level based on a sequential perception of time is unassailable, because time is a necessary ingredient in all human activity. The clock never stops ticking; hours pass away regardless of what we do. The illusion of time and space I am referring to is that of any particular explanation being yours alone and based on your point of view. (Physicists point out, by the way, that there is no big clock in the universe that makes it a particular time in the sense of a clock. Clock time is completely relative, as is clear from time zones on earth. Clock time and dates primarily serve the human purposes of allowing us to coordinate our activities, measure how long something takes, and have a sense of changing seasons).

Even when you have directly observed something, your sequence of explaining what happened before is subjective. An unfortunate and famous case of this is the tape of the beating of Los Angeles motorist Rodney King. African Americans viewing the tape saw a completely different sequence of events than white police officers (as evident in the riots following the court decision in this case). The point at which an observer felt Mr. King was subdued (and, therefore, at which time the officers were out of danger and should have stopped beating him) varied by observer. Who we are (our values, our beliefs, our feelings, and other things about us) somehow muddies the waters of our perception of the order in which things are happening and should happen.

A company that clearly must have stepped outside of the "this before that" trap has to be the Kajima Corporation of Japan. This company knocks down buildings. On the surface, knocking down a building appears to be a simple thing—you figure out a way to topple the whole structure from top to bottom. Kajima takes a different approach; it uses what it calls a "cut and take down" method in which the bottom floors are taken out one at a time. It literally supports the whole structure and destroys the building level by level *from the bottom up*. Using hot pink struts, it supports the building so that it can be taken down one level at a time (see: http://www.boingboing.net/2008/07/14/building-demolition.html). The benefits are that this approach dramatically cuts down on the amount of dust and debris spread in the surrounding area, makes a lot less noise pollution, and allows for a lot more material to be recovered and recycled (Kajima claims to reclaim an average of 92% of the materials from the interiors of buildings). Clearly, the company is not just a demolition company, but a sustainable reclamation company as well. Demolishing a building for Kajima has multiple purposes in a multilevel strategy.

In many instances, especially when working with groups to create a set of scenarios to guide their planning, the key events that drive the scenario over time must be described. The conversation is "this" leads to "that." The question of plausibility guides this process—"Is X plausible or realistic?" Very often, a few people dominate this creative process, or, more commonly, some anchoring event and sequence seems inviolate for the group. This holding onto and believing the sequence often moves into taking positions. The arguments for those positions are always presented in a manner that seems grounded in reality.

In industry, very often there are lockstep rules such as, "Customer demand will shift only when prices change; therefore to get people to buy more or less we must change (lower or raise) prices. Prices change and then consumers change." But this view is regularly proven wrong when customers change consumption patterns based on other things, such as style, safety, or the availability of better alternatives. Price can clearly be a factor in consumption, but not the only one that predicts the order of events in the market. Another lockstep rule in some industries is to slowly evolve a successful product so the customer is not surprised. The flaw in this kind of thinking has been pinpointed especially well in the insightful book *The Innovators Dilemma,* by Clayton Christensen. A competitor (either direct or indirect) may jump ahead by meeting the existing and unacknowledged new needs and desires of the customer. Believing the customer is stuck in a time-sequence of thinking about having his or her needs and desires met can be clearly misleading. For example, I don't think that, when Hewlett-Packard reinvented printing and brought it into the computer age, a cheaper, faster version of the IBM Selectric typewriter would have been a great innovation.

Very often in planning meetings the discussion goes something like this: "We have to do *this* before we can do *that*; we have to crawl before we can walk." Such advice is often wise and a great way to manage risks. However, creativity might be released if there were room for questions such as, "Do we have to do *this* before *that*?" Or, "Can we do *this* at the same time as *that*?"

Out of the Blue

This aspect of quantum physics also points out that something can suddenly emerge at a time and place when it had not been there an instant before. This is an important second aspect of this time-and-space idea that touches on innovation and catalytic events. In many cases, something can seemingly emerge from nowhere and change everything. The reason *this* does not have to follow *that* is that something can emerge out of nowhere and completely change what the perceived order is; the old order becomes instantly irrelevant.

I want to be careful here and not imply that physical objects can emerge from nowhere and hit you on the head, or that factors can appear in the marketplace and be completely untraceable. What I am suggesting is that some new thing can emerge swiftly and change perceptions, and thereby instantaneously make the business environment very different. The "coming out of nowhere" of a new product or service is not the thing to note. What is important to note is the shift in the business environment or market that occurs afterward. The most important aspect of the change is not simply the "hard facts" aspects, but the change in perceptions and attitudes of key stakeholders (customers and other competitors in particular) related to the "hard facts." For an example, let's return to the Toyota Prius automobile: The entry of this car (after many years of hard work by Toyota engineers, no doubt) instantly changed what was possible in the following ways: A car that was not entirely driven by an internal combustion engine could be feasible and reliable. A high-mileage car could be made available at a reasonable price. Another level on lower environmental impacts became possible. A different driving experience (much quieter and with a different information interface—mileage possible on the level of the battery charge) was made possible. Toyota took a very significant risk at the time because there was very little evidence that consumers would buy such a vehicle in large numbers. In fact, based on gasoline prices at the time, the vehicle was uneconomical. But the rewards of taking that risk have been substantial: Toyota is now in the lead with this technology and the consumer experience with it. Every other car company that may have thought it had time to decide when or if to enter the hybrid-car market has had to recalibrate based on the success of Toyota. Perceptions and attitudes changed not only within the companies, but also with customers and other key stakeholders in the industry, such as regulators (notice the push toward higher mileage standards at the national level).

Thinking as an economist, I see the following ways something can appear seemingly out of nowhere.

1. *Technology breakthroughs directly related to an industry's product or service:* a technological innovation occurs that makes new capabilities possible for meeting the needs and desires that the product or service is fulfilling (think color printers versus typewriters). This breakthrough then changes the competitive balance and the concept of what

is possible in the minds of customers of that product or service. Often this breakthrough comes from investing time and resources, so it is not literally from "nowhere." The "nowhere" aspect is related to the discovery process (an "aha!" on the part of researchers) and the sudden change in customer expectations of what is possible. History is full of examples of this kind of shift (a good example is from typewriters to personal computers and printers) and they are easy to see from looking at the companies and organizations who failed because they could not adjust.

2. *Technology breakthroughs indirectly related to an industry's product or service:* a breakthrough from another field impacts on an industry because there are advantages from using it (lowering costs, adding features, improving service, etc.). An example that is affecting almost every industry is the rise of the Internet. The Internet actually came into being from adding new ideas on how to use communications, software, and computers. Since its introduction, with its incredible economics and features, it has changed our world. Another example from outside an industry was the impact of video recording (VCRs, DVDs) on the motion picture business. Video recording shifted the economics; major revenue streams moved from being based primarily on theater releases (which still matter) to deriving substantially from video distribution to the home.

3. *An out-of-the-blue impact on an industry* can also occur when there is a significant (often structural) change in an *unrelated industry*, which leads to spillover effects in another. For example, the high price of gasoline during the first half of 2008 had a major impact on the public transportation sector as people began to drive a lot less. In many cities, public transportation agencies were unprepared for the sharp rise in ridership. The motel industry was also impacted by higher gasoline prices as people made fewer long trips by car. High gasoline prices have been driven by a host of factors, including rising global demand from emerging countries like China and India, as well as concerns

about terrorist attacks and energy security. For a local motel manager or public transportation manager, events in China and India seem far afield, and the sequence of how events in China and India can lead to changes in their industries clearly defies any lockstep thinking.

4. *A shift in values that changes behavior can also cause a big change to come out of the blue.* This kind of shift is readily visible in trends in tastes in music, clothing, and other areas open to fashion or style. Fashion and style are direct inventions of the mind and are on the leading edge of the creative process. Political shifts that get translated into new tax policies, regulations, and rules can also emerge from seemingly overnight changes in values and have significant impacts on businesses of all sorts. Though clearly building on the long heritage of the environmental movement in the U.S. and in the world at large, the movie *An Inconvenient Truth,* about global climate change, had a huge impact over the course of a single year on changing political values toward addressing the issue. Again the key thing to note is the change in perceptions and attitudes about the "facts," even when they may be in dispute. No lockstep of a "this" after a certain "that" is required.

Planning, Modeling, and the Illusion of Time and Space

Letting go of a view of an unchangeable sequence for something to happen will open new ways to think more creatively. Being willing to see any order of events, no matter how tightly held and believed, as just one possibility, *and that there are others,* can open up space for thinking. Acknowledging a locked-in position on a sequence can also pinpoint where there may be big risks should it prove wrong. Examples exist in failures in the investment fund industry (see *When Genius Failed, the Rise and Fall of Long-Term Capital Management,* by Roger Lowenstein, and *The Economist,* August 9–13, 2008, "Confessions of a

Risk Manager," page 72–73, no author listed) because leveraged bets are made on patterns of relationships between markets and securities. There is generally a well-researched record of those relationships that quantify the past in great detail. What always resists research is the sudden new thing that upsets the old relationships. When this happens, fortunes can be lost in an instant.

Having built a few quantitative models for planning purposes in my career, I know that models are brittle in the sense that assumptions and sequences are hardened into equations. The order in the equations of what is added to, or subtracted from, or divided by becomes a hard sequence. Move one thing out of sequence and the entire analysis can be upset. Very often a core assumption in a planning model is that a key sequence *cannot* change. The unchanging nature of the assumption is generally based on historical observations.

Here are some ways to use this time-and-space-illusion idea to help open up planning and bring in more creativity.

1. Find places in planning deliberations where there is an important time-ordered sequence.

2. Investigate the assumptions behind that sequence and challenge those assumptions.

3. Use new assumptions to change the sequence just to see what can be learned.

4. Imagine what "impossible" things might occur out of the blue that may violate the sequence or make it irrelevant.

5. Investigate both the downsides and the upsides of such a violation of the sequence.

Relaxing the constraint of time-sequence helps open up space for alternative views of the same world. Chapter 7 suggests ways to see totally new worlds.

Personal notes and ideas

Examples for my industry

Examples from other industries

Potential good questions

CHAPTER

7

Many Worlds: Catalytic and Kaleidoscopic Thinking

QUANTUM PHYSICS SUGGESTS THAT a different point of observation will lead to a different position for a light particle or a different probability. This seems like a very simple statement and could be mistakenly summed up in a very limited way as suggesting that things are different according to how you look at them. I think it says a lot more, and the key point is in the meaning of the last three words—a different probability. What this says is that a change in perspective not only changes how we see things, but what is possible.

Holding Space Open for Something New

Change one thing and it might lead to a whole new world. This calls to mind what happens when we look inside a kaleidoscope; just a slight shift and movement of one particle can change the whole picture, revealing a new one just as beautiful and breathtaking as the vision before the change. This kind of change is beyond what is defined as

Chapter Overview

Idea from Physics

A different point of observation will lead to a different position for a light particle or a different probability of its speed. Two simultaneous observations from different points can give different, true, and accurate measurements. A change in the rate of vibration of a particle can make it appear or disappear.

Idea Translated for Planning

There are multiple *and* internally consistent ways to perceive and describe events and trends in the business environment or marketplace. Multiple points of view can be held and used as the basis for forming different ideas and intentions. Competitors, regulators, customers, and other stakeholders/outsiders may observe the same set of events and trends and draw very different, and equally valid, perceptions. New observations can change how the business environment is perceived and lead to different strategies and actions by all players.

Applications for Planning

» Actively seek out alternative perspectives—from both outsiders and those you dislike or disagree with.

» Brainstorm a list of ideas or events that seem to be on the periphery but may have potentially large impacts on your organization. Learn more about them.

» Legitimize a process in your planning in which completely "out-of-the-blue" events are put on the table. Find possible out-of-the-blue events through a diverse, knowledgeable, and well-informed group of outsiders.

» Integrate wild cards and outliers into scenario analyses, and use them to generate innovative and creative ideas and strategies.

possible simply by adjusting the time sequence of events in the *same* world. Change in this case results in a completely *new world altogether.*

In organizing one's thinking about a complex business environment, there is often a need to minimize and simplify the number of factors that matter. Limiting focus eases comprehension of what is there. I have often witnessed pushing toward simplification in statements such as, "If we have the best technology at the lowest cost, we will beat the competition." Good technology and cost competitiveness are certainly important factors, but in focusing on them or other so-called key factors, often we divert attention from the many sources of creativity, innovation, and potential change. This kind of oversimplification disconnects the thinking of an organization from its entrepreneurial and creative roots and leads to ignorance driven by a thinking process that ignores things that have hidden and emerging potential. It leads to discounting what appear to be small developments that can and do have big and catalytic potential.

The knowledge that something emerges from nothing is actually something we experience every day in music. It is interesting to note that Einstein was also a very good violinist. When listening to my favorite piece of music that really gets me moving (and I recommend you try this with one of your favorite songs), I reflect on the fact that this great tune actually emerged from a composer's imagination. It started off somewhere between the composer's head and heart. After playing around with it and listening to a deeper place within him or her, the composer *got it.* I can imagine a high level of vibration starting off in the composer's imagination as just a small tune, maybe inspired by nature or street sounds. If it is a piece to be played by a band, then it must be shared with other instrumentalists, and, eventually, the whole thing comes together. One of the great pieces of music in jazz history is *Kind of Blue* by Miles Davis and a quintet of jazz greats. It is one take of improvised jazz that literally comes from mind and heart to the ear. It is also a great example of catalytic and kaleidoscopic creation because each piece starts with a theme and then others interpret it. It is pure creativity captured for us to enjoy.

One my favorite stories about how small things can have a catalytic and kaleidoscopic impact is captured in the rise of televised poker games. Poker is an old game and has been played for decades in homes, garages, and back alleys. Why all of a sudden, around 1997, did it explode onto television and become a multimillion-dollar phenomenon? It all started with the invention by Henry Orenstein of a small set of cameras imbedded in the poker table that allow viewers to see what cards players are holding. Mr. Orenstein was a successful toy manufacturer, not a television producer. He stated in an interview for the *New York Times*, "Before, you never knew who had what cards. Now you can see strategy in the middle of the game." This single change tapped into the already wide love of the game by players and has made millionaires and celebrities out of people who previously had very ordinary lives and very ordinary jobs. With advertising, game winnings, sale of computer-related games, and the impact it has had on visitors to the hotels and casinos hosting the events, televised poker is now a multibillion-dollar industry. The catalyst was the camera; a kaleidoscopic response was created when the entertainment industry tapped into a fertile and not yet fully exploited love of the game of poker, and the human attraction to risk-taking and gambling. When put together with the marketing prowess of the producers at the Fox Television and ESPN networks, the television-poker phenomenon quickly took shape. That such an explosive business should emerge from the tinkering mind of a retiring toy-company owner was surely a long shot. The television networks that first took the risk went in lightly with a few broadcasts at late hours. The initial ratings were beyond what they expected and the rest is history.

What this story highlights for me, for strategic planning, is that holding space for the extraordinary is how the growth of the organization might be possible. It argues for holding a space in the planning process for seemingly small, insignificant ideas held by a fringe or small group (maybe even one person). It suggests a deeper study of how the interconnectedness of large and small factors plays in the business environment and can influence an organization's success. An emergent event, in combination with a change in perspective, can create entirely new possibilities.

This story also suggests how wide the net might be cast to understand what can be a catalytic event that changes a business environment. A camera expands the popularity of the game of poker and creates a new industry—not an obvious and direct connection. There are parallels in many other industries where "something over there changes something over here" and changes the whole business environment. I see a few examples in the following areas, especially where digital technology is changing our world.

1. The invention of the Internet and e-commerce, where online sites such as amazon.com and megastores such as Barnes & Noble contributed to the closure of local bookstores.

2. The rise of personal digital cameras and the YouTube website, which are changing the television news business in terms of breaking news stories and influencing public opinion.

3. The cheaper lease financing of airplanes, leading to guaranteed overnight mail and package delivery nationwide (check the history of Federal Express).

This kind of catalytic and kaleidoscopic thinking demands planning based on what is "not there yet." There can be no predetermined, verifiable proof, only a good story full of potential surprises. Imagine the story Henry Orenstein had to tell the producers at ESPN! "This little camera can make you millions of dollars!" Imagine the change in perspective about what might constitute good sports television for people accustomed to televising football, baseball, and basketball games. Returning to quantum physics, a new perspective also alters the possibility of where an electron might be. What is possible becomes different *because* of the change in perspective. What this means in organizations is that a change in perspective changes the potential of what the organization can become. Even one person "seeing it" might be sufficient. Change can start with one person "seeing it" and getting others to consider the possibilities. A dimly seen possibility can become real as other people think it has a higher probability. At the point of "seeing," all possibilities have the same probability. How a possibility becomes real is based on bringing together both controllable and uncontrollable factors. Clear intention and action must follow in all cases. Learning and adjustments in implementing the vision occur in all cases.

Often in organizations people are not allowed to be imaginative and can share their imaginative stories with only a few limited and trusted colleagues (often outside work hours). When groups are doing strategic planning, imagination is often not only discouraged but might lead to a career-limiting experience. People sharing the imaginative ideas are often risking derision and criticism. Telling a story in which you suggest that latent forces might emerge in new ways to support your idea may even be viewed as unintelligent because the tale resists the kind of lockstep logic people are trained to expect. We all know one person can make a difference; it is just often too hard for someone to break the mold in most organizations.

Catalytic and kaleidoscopic thinking also emphasizes the fluidity and constant amount of change that is always going on, and how persistently looking at things from many different angles and perspectives is necessary. This kind of thinking certainly is made easier by having a diversity of people, backgrounds, kinds of expertise, and thought in a planning process. It also demands deep listening skills that accentuate openness, and understanding a perspective before unusual ideas are too quickly judged. While listening, one cannot be building a case to prove the other person wrong. Looking at things in an open way, and listening at a deeper level, must be accompanied by a willingness to change one's mind and move away from positionality.

Making a Safe Place for Catalytic and Kaleidoscopic Thinking in Planning

It will not be easy to achieve catalytic and kaleidoscopic thinking in most organizations because many people simply will not make the time. However, one or all of the following processes can be done, in more or less detail, before or during a planning process.

1. Make an explicit part of the planning process open for wild cards. Set ground rules for this time that encourage openness, neutrality, and support. Criticism and negative inputs should be off-limits. People should be encouraged to think about weak signals of change and outliers. These wild cards should be put in story form and shared. A good reference for the use of stories in organizations is *The Power of the Tale: Using Narratives for Organisational Success,* by Julie Allan, Gerard Fairtlough, and Barbara Heinzen.

2. Set aside time to brainstorm the intangible factors that are important to the success of your organization or that play in the organization's business environment. Don't worry about having a complete list, but don't settle for fewer than five; more than ten may be too many. Intangibles include such things as the organization's reputation, how it is perceived by

key parties (customers, suppliers, or competitors), its ability to attract good people, and/or the ease of use of its products or services. If time allows, people can be encouraged to think of stories in which the intangibles become a primary concern in the organization's future plans.

3. Get clear on the needs or desires your products or services are meeting for your customers that are core to the value you provide. Brainstorm ways those needs and desires might be met in completely different ways. Come up with at least two stories that seem to "break the rules" and rely on something emerging that doesn't currently exist. (For example, I can imagine the iPod emerging out of projections for really cheap and powerful memory chips and digital processors.)

These tasks, though probably time-consuming, I think will become more important as our economy and lives become more globally interconnected. Global interconnections will make the really big picture even bigger. I turn to the really big picture in Chapter 8.

Personal notes and ideas

Examples for my industry

Examples from other industries

Potential good questions

Thinking and Planning in the Field of All Possibilities

As I write this book, I have suddenly become very concerned about you the reader. As it turns out, you will now become my competitor. I sincerely hope that by this point you have made a lot of valuable notes in the margins and in the pages provided for you at the end of each chapter to capture your ideas. This will also be an indication that you liked the book and might recommend it to others so that they can make their own notes. I hope you have personalized the book so that it is uniquely valuable to you. If you have done so, there is a lower likelihood that you will sell this book on the Internet through some used-book site and thereby compete directly with me and my publisher. We are now economically connected.

Chapter Overview

Idea from Physics

Everything is connected in a unified field and in balance. The totality of all the powers in the field causes all of existence to come into reality at any given moment.

Idea Translated for Planning

The whole business environment in which the organization exists is one interconnected place. Everything and anything might have some influence on the business environment and thus the success of the organization. There are weak and strong forces influencing the business environment and they are always interacting in a way that seeks balance. Over time, those forces will change and the balance in the business environment will shift.

Applications for Planning

» Accept and become comfortable with the fact that the entire company, its people, its products and services, its relationships—everything about it—are connected either weakly or strongly to everything in its business environment.

» At the beginning of the planning process, clarify how the organization views itself in the context of the uncertainty it faces.

» Compile a working list of both strong and weak forces that influence the business environment in which the organization exists. Use this list in strategic assessments or scenario analyses as part of a learning process.

» Focus on factors that contribute to how the organization uses and absorbs new ideas and how it adapts its structure. Create a balanced scorecard analysis around those factors as a part of strategic planning. Capture what is learned for creativity and innovation.

Connection and Interaction As the Core of the Business Environment

I have created a wonderful website (www.artofquantumplanning.com) for you and me to continue and to extend our connection. Your ideas will soon begin to shape mine and make me much smarter. You, I, and other readers will share our learning with each other when you visit my site. So you are not just my competitor, you are also my partner in learning and sharing the ideas of this book.

It is highly likely that I will learn entirely new things as I interact with you, the reader. I may learn something that might change my life. I may learn something that encourages me to write a sequel to this book that goes in an entirely new direction. I have no idea what to expect. I have no idea who I might meet and becomes friends with as a result of this book. I may meet people from many countries. My best choice is to be open to everyone.

The interconnection between you and me in my small business of being an author (best-selling, I hope!) has a chance to create echoes all over the business world. I believe the entire world of business is being reshaped by the forces of interconnection, transparency, and coordination being made possible by computer, software, and communications technologies. There are no longer any barriers to keep these forces at bay. These forces are now inseparable from the business environment. What these forces may make possible, in terms of change and innovation driven by much faster learning by all humankind, is impossible to forecast. The business environment itself has become a learning and living entity.

I believe some very wonderful things will become possible when we all become co-creators with the producers of just about everything we consume. It is now possible, with many products, to directly communicate with the creators of them and make suggestions (solicited or unsolicited). In addition to digital consumer products such as the iPhone, this co-creative process is also true in the media business with TV shows, movies, videogames, and books. Fans now play a big role in product evolution. As consumer co-creation and productive connection moves to other products and services, creativity will continue to explode and with it innovation.

My point in this chapter is not to loosely or wildly argue that everything is possible. Recall that quantum physics demands that the system must be in balance. Out-of-balance situations can lead to crashes to reestablish balance. Where new thinking is needed is in expanding the range of positions that can be in balance; they extend far beyond our narrow positions and perspectives, which are often based on dualistic thinking. Additionally, our participations, attitudes, and actions directly affect the state of the balance *in a continuous feedback loop.* Staying open to the continuous flow of information from the feedback loop is critical.

With such a wide range of possibilities at any instant and the interconnection of it all, how then does one plan? If the field of possibility is in such constant flux and continually rebalancing, then how does one think about such variability and set a clear intention? If the total business environment can never be fully known, is there any use to planning at all? I say, "Yes." The reason to plan is to learn and master change. The role of planning is to support organizational learning and build flexibility to adapt to change as a competitive advantage. Planning's job is to create an interactive and continuous learning process that will strengthen the adaptability of the organization to a changing environment.

Perspective and Planning in an Environment of Unrelenting Global Change

In my experience with planning teams, there is often no clearly understood and agreed-upon way that the team sees the company in relation to the uncertainty faced in the business environment. Are the company and the team helpless? Is there a clear and shared intention that can be used to focus energy into the business environment? Can the organization exert any influence on the business environment to balance it in a certain way that will benefit the company? The answers to these questions are keys to better planning results.

In the uncertainty in the field of all possibilities, I see three approaches to planning that explicitly position the company in relation to how it perceives uncertainty in the business environment. These approaches capture what position (or self-perception) underlies your planning based on your overriding view of the uncertainty you face in the business environment.

The First Approach: RFAF (Ready-Fire-Aim-Fire)

You, or your team in leading planning, see the field of all possibilities and ask, "Will the conditions that emerge in the business environment (field) allow what we want to create to come into existence?" In business this question could be translated as, "Are business conditions (which we don't control) going to evolve in a way that will allow our business (products and services) to prosper?" In this case, there is a sense of "let's try it and see what happens, and we believe we have a good chance." Look, invest, learn, invest some more; this is the RFAF track. If you were planning, for example, to open a restaurant in San Francisco, you might have this as an approach and worldview. You might believe that it will not pay to try to analyze an uncontrollable and highly uncertain environment, so you just dive in and learn by doing. Often when a powerful CEO is doing most of the planning, this way of thinking is that person's underlying psychological position. This can work well if the CEO is open to constant learning and is very careful about taking positions.

The Second Approach: ARFA (Aim-Ready-Fire-Aim)

The second approach to planning in relation to an uncertain business environment is based on seeing the field of all possibilities and asking: "What is likely to come into existence based on how I see the field emerging, and how do I take advantage of it?" In business this gets translated as, "I expect business conditions to move in a particular direction, so what can the business create to take advantage of those conditions?" Here the disadvantage of not controlling market conditions is ignored because there is an intention. In this case, there is a sense of "let's try to catch a wave we expect is coming!" It is strategy by anticipation—anticipating needs and desires of customers, or even competitive or economic conditions. I can imagine this kind of thinking driving Apple into the cell phone and personal digital assistant market. Learn, look, invest, and then learn some more is the ARFA track.

The Third Approach: ACRF (Aim-Control-Ready-Fire)

The third approach to planning, with such massive uncertainty in the business environment, is to start with the question "How do we exert will, or intentionality, on the field to contribute to conditions arising that allow the business conditions we desire to come into existence?" In business, this might be translated into questions such as "How do we attempt to affect business conditions so that they play to our advantage?" and "How can we be catalytic and change the balance of forces in the market?" Here the disadvantage of not controlling market conditions is not the focus of attention. Having a strong intention is the focus. The organization is not planning to take advantage of expected conditions, but literally to influence the desired conditions so that they arise. Intention is accompanied by action that supports an investment. Learn, look, control some of the environment and then invest is the ACRF track. Among the ways companies pursue this approach are influencing laws and regulations, controlling and introducing breakthrough technology, creating a strong brand identity for which there is no substitute, and having trade barriers put in place; in general, all four ways are aimed at erecting barriers to competition in the market. Many regulated energy utilities have succeeded in using the approach of influencing regulations and using them to build barriers to competition in their markets. Obviously, many companies attempt to manufacture demand (through advertising and public relations) and erect powerfully protective perceptions in the minds of consumers. To the extent that companies deliver on their advertised promises, they can be very successful.

No particular one of the three approaches, RFAF, ARFA, or ACRF, is always "right" or even better than another. It depends on the company or organization and the conditions in its industry. If there are a large number of competitors in a market, it will generally be tougher (though not impossible) for a single player to influence the business environment. For large companies with multiple product lines, one of the three different approaches may be appropriate for some parts of the business and not for others. For companies in industries with regulated monopolies or oligopolies, influencing market conditions is a normal part of the business environment. The planner's (or the team's) job is to figure this out so that there is clarity in how the larger uncertainty in the business environment is understood.

A fundamental misunderstanding, or lack of a shared understanding, in conceptualizing the business environment can be harmful. When the track from idea to investment is unclear or not widely shared within a company, there is confusion. An underlying confusion on the part of a planning group (often hidden and embedded in the planning process) about how the business environment is viewed can radiate and lead to dissonance throughout the strategy-development process. People may be unconscious of the fact that they are functioning from wholly different assumptions about the nature of the business environment. Often there is no shared understanding of the order of aiming, getting ready, firing, or controlling because there is no shared view of the nature of the business environment or the playing field. I don't mean to pick on Lehman Brothers, but here was a very clear case of a fundamental misunderstanding of a massively changing business environment.

I believe that using an Aim-Fire-Ready-Fire approach is powerful when there is an opportunity for intention and anticipation to combine into an entrepreneurial moment. Both small and large companies cherish those moments of opportunity. It is a goal of a good planning process to find them. Opportunities to use and prosper from catalytic investments are also vital to good business planning and may benefit from a Ready-Fire-Aim approach. If leaders of an organization know or feel they can shape the business environment, the Aim-Control-Ready-Fire approach should be used. However, efforts to erect barriers to competition and innovation, and thereby maintain high cost structures, are poor ways to influence the business environment. In this case the Aim-Control-Ready-Fire approach often gets stuck in the control-ready stage, leading to misfiring. A summary of the three approaches and what they suggest for the strategy and investment process is shown in Figure 1.

Interactive Planning in the Field of All Possibilities

Decisions made in a planning process impact the very field the planners are playing in. Strategic planning decisions are an element of shaping the very business environment for which they are planned. This is one of the most overlooked understandings I have regularly encountered with a planning group. They leave the room, having worked hard,

---

FIGURE 1
WORLDVIEW OF THE COMPLEX BUSINESS ENVIRONMENT

Organizational View	Context of Strategy Formulation and Investment
» Conditions are far too uncertain; resources analysis should be limited.	» Ready-Fire-Aim-Fire (RFAF): Studying the business environment for too long is seen as paralysis and a poor use of limited resources, therefore the bias is toward taking action, learning something and then taking more action. Investing and learning by doing is the underlying belief.
» Complex conditions exist, but we have a clear intention and are willing to interact with changing conditions.	» Aim-Ready-Fire-Aim (ARFA): There is a belief that the business environment is complex and evolving in a certain manner and that a risk can be taken to anticipate conditions and thereby make a profit. Studying the environment is done to give context for anticipating conditions. A powerful intention in combination with anticipation of conditions directs investment and learning.
» Complex conditions exist, but we can influence some of the key factors to limit risks.	» Aim-Control-Ready-Fire (ACRF): There is a belief that in the business environment, though it is complex, some factors can be controlled. Studying the environment drives the selection of which factors to seek to control. A clear intention combined with efforts to limit downside risks (or to secure advantage) directs investment and learning.

---

thinking they are about to take actions that will not have a feedback-loop *on their companies,* and thus they fail to acknowledge a need for continued learning and change in response to their own actions. George Soros in *The Crisis of Global Capitalism, Open Society Endangered,* captures this idea as follows:

> *The world in which we live is extremely complicated. To form a view of the world that can serve as a basis for decisions, we must simplify. Using generalizations, metaphors, analogies, comparisons, dichotomies, and other mental constructs serves to introduce some order onto an otherwise confusing universe. But every mental construct distorts to some extent what it represents and every distortion adds something to the world that we need to understand. The more we think, the more we have to think about. This is because reality is not a given. It is formed in the same process as the participant thinking. The more complex the thinking, the more complicated the reality becomes. Thinking can never quite catch up with reality. Reality is always richer than our comprehension. Reality has the power to surprise thinking, and thinking has the power to create reality.*

Certainly planners understand that the plan is not the end of the process but only in rare cases do they see their plans as *learning tools* to better understand the business environment by monitoring the impact of their own organization's actions in addition to those of competitors and other key players, such as regulators. Rarely is there a reflective learning loop built into an ongoing planning process. Very often strategists see themselves metaphorically as making moves on a chessboard—they make a move, then someone else makes a move in response in some orderly fashion. If they were to extend this metaphor, they might see that after they make the first move, the next move will not just be another single piece moving in response, but that the other player cheats and moves several pieces in response, and that even *occasionally a nonplayer changes some of the spaces on the board as well.* Strategic actions not only change how competitors might respond but can also have an impact on the larger business environment (i.e., they may impact perceptions about what is possible and impact related industries, causing strong or weak feedback loops).

An example of this kind of field-wide thinking in strategy is currently playing out in the energy sector around new battery technology. As more research is being done on the batteries that are making hybrid vehicles perform better, those discoveries (and their related economics of scale and production) will flow into other sectors of the energy-storage market and eventually change how energy is supplied, stored, and used in other areas (e.g., emergency backup systems, and other off-the-power-grid applications such as road signs and recreation).

The few cases in which I have seen planners think about the feedback loops and their strategies have been in organizations with a very strong marketing influence in top leadership. Companies in very fast-changing competitive markets are more likely to plan in a way that keeps them looking for market responses to their moves. In some cases, companies are able to read these signals and see other potential opportunities (a review of the history of Post-It Notes, by the 3M Company, is a good example).

Understanding Balance in Planning in the Field of All Possibilities

Having a clear approach to how one sees the organization in relation to the field of all possibilities in the business environment (and coming to a consensus) is a good first step. It might relieve a lot of confusion. However, once moving in that field and interacting and adjusting in the process of readying, firing, aiming, and attempting control, what comes next? Is there any other guidance? I think the concept of being in balance with some big forces in the environment and steadily rebalancing deserves some thought.

I am familiar with the concept of the balanced scorecard as originally introduced in the book *The Balanced Scorecard* by Robert S. Kaplan and David P. Norton in 1996. The idea of expanding business and strategic management beyond financial measures and into operational measures, and ones that capture organizational learning, is clearly sound. Lots of good work has been done here. There may be room for some creative work using the quantum principles I have outlined in this book to expand the concept of a balanced scorecard. I don't think there will be one answer in such an approach for all organizations, because the balanced scorecard is generally customized in actual application.

Acknowledging the need for customization, I have two suggestions for the balanced-scorecard approach. First, returning to the ideas of Chapter 2, where I suggested seeing organizations as energy systems, a balanced-scorecard approach can be used to assess the flow of energy in the business. Second, as I have argued previously about the role of planning to build in flexibility, a balanced-scorecard approach could be targeted at finding measures to assess the adaptability of the organization. Figure 2 highlights these two suggestions.

As much as I think that a lot of value can be found in the steps we have just covered, my personal experience in strategic planning has taught me that there is more to it than going through the mental and analytical steps properly. I think working toward balance in an organization is more than just doing a well-structured analysis with lots of good quantification. Strategic planning is not just a job, but a wealth-creating process that not only enriches owners, but provides a better life for the people using the organization's products and services.

FIGURE 2

QUANTUM IDEAS AND THE BALANCED SCORECARD

Ease of Business Flow

» Look for quantitative and qualitative measures of how key aspects of business operations are conducted in a flowing and easy manner. If the company is indeed an energy system, then energy should not be blocked. Key areas to assess might include the ease of customer access to the product or service offered, and the movement of key inputs of production.

» Find ways to assess the ease of communication flows in key areas of the business that drive value creation. The flow of ideas is the thinking process of the business. Key areas to assess include connections between marketing/business development and research and development.

Level of Flexibility and Changeability

» Look for quantitative and qualitative ways to assess the ability of the organization to make changes in the use of soft assets (e.g., labor, financial resources) and hard assets (e.g., buildings and equipment) that will support creation of new value in products or services.

» Find ways to lower the cost of and other impediments to transformation. This should include not only changing structural elements, but also such intangibles as organizational culture, the knowledge resources of the company and the flexibility of the workforce and its skill base.

I am not convinced that good planning (much less breakthrough-level planning) can be done by persons or teams who are themselves out of balance. Planning is a human process, so I think we all have a tool that can help us achieve balance if we choose to use it—our heart.

As you know by now, I spent many years working in and consulting to the electric power industry. I did this in the U.S. and internationally. I was working in the industry during the time of the Enron Corporation financial collapse. I met several Enron executives during this time and generally found them overly self-assured. As is now widely reported, the collapse of the company was foreseen by Sherron S. Watkins, who served as vice president of corporate development. She was at least by title and position a person who was concerned about the future of the company. A key point in Enron's collapse is marked by a letter she wrote to her chairman questioning accounting practices that she feared were hiding losses and inflating profits. Clearly, the company was out of balance. In my view, her courage in stepping forward was an act of her heart as well as her intellect. In my view, she is one of the greatest strategic planners ever because she was one of the most courageous. I think it was something in her heart that drove the right analysis. Her personal sense of balance, in my view, had to play some role.

Returning to the question of balance in the field of all possibilities, as planners I feel we need to find a way to combine the heart and the intellect. The following quote captures the essence of how to do this. It comes from *Think and Grow Rich,* by Napoleon Hill, and it is the fifth factor in his self-confidence formula:

> *I fully realize that no wealth or position can long endure,*
> *unless built upon truth and justice; therefore I will engage in*
> *no transaction which does not benefit all whom it affects. I will*
> *succeed by attracting to myself the forces I wish to use, and the*
> *cooperation of other people. I will induce others to serve me*
> *because of my willingness to serve others. I will eliminate hatred,*
> *envy, jealousy, selfishness, and cynicism by developing love for all*
> *humanity, because I know that a negative attitude toward others*
> *can never bring me success. I will cause others to believe in me*
> *because I will believe in them, and in myself.*

After this statement, Hill's next sentence in the book reads, "Back of this formula is a law of nature, which no man has yet been able to explain."

I think the balancing that needs to be done at this point is not a balancing that takes place solely in the mind of the planner, but in the heart. When I read Hill's fifth factor, the words go to my heart. Truth and justice are things that have to be measured in the heart *and* the mind. A business that has as a core goal to benefit "all whom it affects" must have a vision and concept of itself that extends beyond the narrow interests of profit and beating competitors. Thinking in a planning process about all whom the business affects should open new vistas of ideas and potential strategies.

I see an important connection between the field of all possibilities and the courage and ability to hold a vision that incorporates the word "all." In quantum thinking, the word "all" makes sense because all is connected to all. The field contains all and connects all and keeps all in balance. Quantum thinking and planning should incorporate the power of the interconnectedness of all. Touching back on a company like Wikipedia, this makes sense in actual application—an encyclopedia for all, open to editing by, and contributions from, all.

Building on Hill's formula, what if cooperation and a willingness to serve were foundational to any business operation? What if the company values and culture were ones in which all employees were committed to eliminating hatred, envy, jealousy, selfishness, and cynicism—and an emphasis was placed instead on positive attitudes toward one another? I don't suggest this lightly, because in many cases I have seen negative personal behavior toward team members undermine the effectiveness of a planning process and thereby contribute directly to poor results and harm to the organization. I have seen leaders treat people below them with contempt and do harm to the implementation of strategy and actions by generating fear of punishment. Having an attitude of love and respect toward others, and believing in them, clearly leads to better team results whether in doing planning or playing baseball. Certainly in any organization that has as a part of its vision the incorporation of a sense of all, cooperation and a willingness to serve will be vital to success.

I don't believe quantum leaps in strategic thinking can occur or long endure in organizations in which human relationships are out of balance from a metaphysical standpoint. The process of moving from ideas to action to actualization is a human process that demands connection at the heart level. Playing well in the field of all possibilities cannot be done successfully without the heart, and the heart in balance with the mind. I think some companies understand this and put their CEOs in advertising to give the company a face and a heart. I still warmly recall when Wendy's Old Fashioned Hamburgers put their CEO, "Dave," in their commercials. I felt someone actually cared about the quality of the hamburgers.

Chapter 9 will also address the organization as a whole. It speaks to the energy of an organization, as I see it, from translating how physics sees energy.

Personal notes and ideas

Examples for my industry

Examples from other industries

Potential good questions

9

Organizations As Energy Systems

I SEE A BUSINESS OR ORGANIZATION AS AN ENERGY SYSTEM designed to meet human needs and desires. My colleague Arie de Gues, whom I got to know during my years with GBN, goes as far as to argue that an organization, as a collective entity, is literally alive! What if we stopped for a minute and viewed the organizations we work in or visit every day as if they were alive? In *The Living Company* Arie says,

> *Like all organisms, the living company exists primarily for its own survival and improvement: to fulfill its potential and to become as great as it can be.*

Businesses and Organizations as Energy Systems

What if we saw our companies and organizations as pulsing, wiggling, constantly adjusting, breathing entities? We don't really know what energizes us to breathe every second; we just call it "life." What if

Chapter Overview

Idea from Physics

Everything in the universe is composed of energy. The frequency or vibration level of the energy makes a difference in the form a particular thing takes.

Idea Translated for Planning

Your organization has energy. Your organization is alive and should be viewed as such. The level of energy can rise and fall and affect the state of your organization. The energy level is based on the ideas and values in your organization and how they are positively related through how operating assets are managed to meet the needs of customers. Easing access for customers to get the values they want from your company's offerings will increase your organization's energy level. The energy level will rise by attraction from customers.

Applications for Planning

» Do not think about the organization as an "it" or an inanimate object.

» See and speak of the organization in a way that recognizes its ideas, values, and people as central.

» Make the flexibility and adaptability of the organization an important strategic objective.

» Find ways to build flexibility and adaptability into key operational assets for the primary purpose of improving customer access to the values they want.

we focused on the underlying power circulating through our organizations? What if we looked beyond the balance sheet, the hard assets, the buildings and equipment and asked, "What is causing all of this to be energized and used by people to create something of value?" How would we describe this energizing force? In our physics equations, what would we equate with c^2? How could we use both particle and wave characteristics to find parallels to help us understand how our organizations work on a deeper level?

I think my suggestions in the following paragraphs may serve as a helpful guide and a place to start. But again, some value can be gained from holding the questions above in *your* mind and thinking about (mentally playing with) your organization and going beyond my suggestions.

Ideas As Particles

Organizations start with an idea or several related ideas. The entrepreneurial flash of inspiration is an idea, or a mix of mutually supporting ideas. Planning and establishing all the parts and functions of an organization at its inception is converting an idea into creativity and reality. When companies are struggling and failing, very often the question surfaces, "Anyone with any ideas?" Ideas are little pieces of congealed imagination. They are seeds with potential, but not yet in fertile soil.

Very often when I visit a company, restaurant, or any organization, I try to figure out what is the idea of the place. What did the creators have in mind when they started this? Why is it different from another, similar, place?

Think of several businesses you encounter. For example, when I think of the McDonald's food chain, I think of the idea of this place as fast food of consistent quality that is easy to eat. In comparison, when I think of Whole Foods Markets, I think of the idea of it as making a healthy lifestyle available to me in everything I eat, drink, or put on or in my body. I am sure these companies have a larger set of interconnected ideas at the core of their company's mission that guide their operations.

But for these ideas to be part of an energy system, they have to be good ideas—they must have some ability to attract the interest of people. The ideas must be good in the sense that they meet some human need or desire. Unattractive ideas have no energy. For example, we now have the technology whereby, each time someone rings your doorbell, you can take their picture and have a hard copy available in seconds. Interested in having one of these?

But are ideas alone sufficient? I think not. So what might be the other c to get our c^2 equation going?

Values As a Wave

Ideas, as is clear in the doorbell example, can't exist without a context of values. Imagine that you were building the American ambassador's residence in Iraq and someone mentioned the idea of the high-technology doorbell with instant print copies of the caller's ID. There might be some interest in that idea because the context has changed, and what is valuable is all of sudden very different. The context now must take into account the war-torn and violent environment. Ideas move with values; they are intimately connected. But as we know, values change as the world and circumstances around us change. We want our ideas to do the same and change with the context.

Going back to McDonald's, in today's health-conscious eating environment, fast food with consistent quality is not enough. Goods from Whole Foods Markets sometimes have a cost premium, but perhaps that would be a deterrent only during a recession as shopper's pocketbooks are a little lighter.

Values are grounded in human experience and culture. They can emerge from just about any experience. They are grounded in beliefs.

Therefore, values don't have to be "rational" (rationality itself is subjective). Human experience, which drives culture and beliefs, is an evolving process; therefore values will always change. A readily visible example of this situation is the constant changes in styles of everything from clothing to cars to furniture to music to almost anything we consume. From moment to moment, as new experiences arise, values will shift. Another way that value shifts can be easily seen is in generational shift. My twenty- and sixteen-year-old sons have very different values from mine in several areas, especially in music. I find some of the lyrics in their hip-hop songs offensive and ignorant; they, on the other hand, find them cool and humorous. They find my jazz songs boring; I find them emotionally moving.

c^2: Ideas Multiplied by Values

A good (or even great) idea that addresses a need or desire that is consonant with the values of the people served is what every successful organization must have at its core. Failing organizations can also be diagnosed using this formula. Note I mentioned "values of the people served." What I want to point out here is that I intend no moral or religious slant; pornography and violent videogames are successful businesses that use this formula in their respective markets as well as Whole Foods Markets does in providing nutritious food. If the customer likes it and it resonates with his or her values, then that is the sweet spot.

The power of this formula is this: visualizing ideas in a positive relationship with values suggests to me that values keep ideas current, fluid, flexible, and adaptable to a changing environment. An idea literally becomes a "good" one in the way it gets actualized within the context of a society's values. Joel Garreau's book *Radical Evolution* is passionate about this and warns against the quick adoption of ideas without social and cultural input from a wide range of people, including average citizens.

However, values without any ideas are infertile. For example, it is a great value to hold that all children should have a first-class education to support them in reaching their full potential. Many organizations trying to live up to this value, including public schools, private schools, charter schools, and education-focused foundation; the list goes on. All are looking for better ideas to add to their values. Ideas and values, connecting and integrating into each other, are the core of what makes creativity real in the world. When the relationship between the two is "multiplicative," in the sense that the combination is greater than the two alone, something special can happen. High-Tech High School in San Diego, California, is doing a great job of this in education. The school is anchored in a hands-on, project-based learning approach. The value that all kids can learn, combined with this hands-on teaching and learning style, has created a great success there with almost all of its kids going on to college and a waiting list of applicants.

Mass, or Assets, Used with Ideas and Values to Create Energy

A friend of mine has built a substantial fortune buying godforsaken real estate and turning a handsome profit through wise investment and great marketing ideas. He essentially puts ideas and his values into these old assets. His values tend to be well appreciated by his clients. He has turned old warehouse space into beautiful loft-style housing loved by artists, and in the process has turned a handsome profit. His values have been centered around such concepts as good location, quality reconstruction, attractive colors, and affordable pricing. He could see all of these assets in, for example, an abandoned warehouse in San Francisco.

This concept is not just true for existing assets, but also for assets that don't exist. Ideas and values have to be "actualized" into real things people can use. A great example of this is Apple's iPod. The iPod exemplifies the idea of portability of music and video, thereby meeting the desire of people to have access to their own content in a mobile and high-quality form (using digital and computer technologies). But the iPod is also a study in art and ease of use, and it has been a great success for the company. I am sure Apple's entry into the phone business with its successful iPhone was based on deep study of the needs and desires (i.e., features) that its customers wanted but that were not available. The best of entrepreneurship is the integration of ideas, values, and assets. Assets clearly can also be soft; soft assets can include such things as brand identity (Coke soft drinks), a solid reputation for reliability (Toyota cars), feelings of happiness and fun (Disney theme parks)—and even people. One way people are converted into key assets is through providing solid training programs that assure top-notch personal service for a company's customers.

Going back to the Trader Joe's in my neighborhood, I see a good example of the whole equation working together to create positive energy. Almost anytime I visit the store it is full of customers and most seem happy to be there. This is despite the fact that this is the only store in the area where the checkout process involves *one* line directed to about 10 checkout stands. The lines can sometimes be 50 people long! So why are we all so happy? I think it is the way the whole store operates as an energy system in some subtle ways. The first thing you see when you enter the store is flowers, which immediately adds warmth. The store is well lit. The staff is always friendly and helpful (I don't have to ask; they ask me pleasantly). The store is always well-stocked, so what I come to get I always find (especially my favorite chocolate-covered treats). I have now learned that when I get into the checkout line, even if it is long, it will move fast. Most of the other customers also know this and have a degree of patience. If the line is moving more slowly than normal or is unusually long, I always see store assistants handing out small samples of something delicious to make the time pass and show appreciation to the customers.

My translation of the $E = mc^2$ equation for Trader Joe's might look like this: *Energy* (for Trader Joe's my version of energy consists of sales, profits, brand identity, and customer loyalty) equals *Mass* (their stores, inventory, location, employees, and systems) times c^2 (for them the idea is convenient access to organic, healthy, and gourmet foods times the values their customers hold for healthier, high-quality food that matches their lifestyle choices).

Going back to the art and simplicity of Apple's iPod, I want to touch on the important role of beauty and art. When the manifestation of ideas and of values comes into form, very often art and beauty result. The artistic expression and beauty of a product or service can often send out an attractive vibration. The balance, flow, and visual impact can validate creativity in a special way and be a means of touching us as humans on a deeper level. There can be an emotional response that comes from deep inside. There is a *wow* that emerges in us in the presence of beauty, art, and simplicity.

Planning As If the Organization Is a Whole Energy System

When it all comes together it is magical; when good ideas are tied positively and effectively to the current values of customers and then brought together in a consumable, easy-to-access form, it is hard not to succeed. I feel something positive when I walk into a well-functioning organization of any kind. There is a great pizza restaurant in my neighborhood; it has been there over 20 years. When I walk into the place, it is generally busy if not crowded. There is a smile on nearly everyone's face, especially the counter service people. They are happy to see me and I am happy to see them. The aromas of the ingredients radiate and penetrate my senses, making my mouth water. I feel relaxed sitting at the counter or waiting in line chatting with other patrons. I literally feel energized in the place. It has a little bit of magic and good energy.

Often what I experience in companies and organizations is that they have lost what this little pizza place has in volumes—energy. What saddens me is that the people who are in charge of changing those companies—the folks involved in planning and charting the future of the organization—have lost touch with what energizes the company. I am not always sure why they have lost touch with it, but I can imagine some of the reasons. People often see their jobs in political terms ("My job is to keep person X happy or to protect person X's interests"). Sometimes people have been doing their jobs for so long and in such a routine fashion that they have lost touch with how the job connects with what matters. Whatever the reason, they are unable to think in a way that energizes or incites some creative spark in their organizations.

I don't think it is solely the planning function that can help an organization be more energized. How people are treated and honored in an organization is a good place to start, and everyone can participate. Treating people with respect and with empathy can go a long way, and respect is sadly absent in many organizations. Without respect, it is easy to see the organization as some kind of "it" responding mechanically. I recall an idea in consulting circles a few years ago about "reengineering" organizations. People I know who experimented with it found that it left out the human component, especially emotional intelligence, and thus did not last long.

Being clear about what values and higher ideals an organization is in existence to serve is often skipped over, forgotten, or not given adequate emphasis. Revisiting and revalidating those values and higher ideals can be a part of the planning process. Effective leaders, I find, don't forget those higher values and often almost embody them by their actions. Many organizations are very effective in rewarding actions and recognizing people who not only embody the organization values but find a way to translate that to other employees and even customers. I was an employee at PG&E during the 1989 San Francisco earthquake. The passion the company's workers put into restoring power, gas, and keeping people safe was so evident that there were thank-you signs all over the city. Customer service really means something!

Making the flexibility and adaptability of the organization an important strategic objective in a company's plan can often get lost in the rush to cut costs. Flexibility can sometimes mean having extra resources that can be used to adapt to change. A lean company may see extra resources as fat and waste and not as a reserve for flexibility. It can be tough to balance extra resources with a lean agenda, especially if resources are already in short supply.

A good place to find the right balance is to look for ways to build flexibility and adaptability into the key operating assets most connected to the primary purpose of improving customer access to the values they want. This will vary in companies, and isolating those areas (and how they might shift over time) can be a key function in the planning process itself. In some companies it may be customer service and in others it may be research and development. It might shift over time from financial management (easing car financing for customers) to engineering and design (hybrid engines and fuel efficiency), as it did in the auto industry over the last decade.

I hope that using the ideas in this chapter can provide a way to recharge your thinking about the core energizing structure of your organization. You can think through the suggestions given or return to the core questions at the beginning of this chapter and play with them to generate answers that are specific to your organization or industry.

Remember the formula $E = mc^2$. The energy (attractive power) of a business is equal to a positive relationship (multiplicative) between productive assets and good creative ideas meeting the values of the people served.

Implementing the Quantum Ideas

I suspect that in pondering the ideas I have been discussing, you have occasionally noted that they have parallels in human relationships. For example, resisting duality can easily relate to not putting people in a "me versus you" position or oversimplifying the totality of a person's talents and gifts. The concept of inescapable uncertainty should place some limits on how sure we can be about anything; and thus, letting go of some positions we hold dearly, can lead to flexibility and open-ness that can smooth human relationships. The illusion of time and space should give us personal pause in our habitual way of thinking (that we know the exact cause and effect of anything), and again open up space for listening to the perspectives of others.

In short, good planning has both personal and social dimensions. The people doing it are human beings! Who is doing the planning, and where they are on their own personal growth path matter. Using the quantum ideas I have been discussing can be easier with some personal reflections. Getting the courage to step up comes from the inside out.

Of course, as I have stated in earlier chapters of this book, I rec-ommend and hope that the leadership of an organization creates, supports, and encourages a learning-oriented environment within the organization. And the spirit of that environment finds its expression in the planning process of the organization. In the event such an environ-ment is not present or perfect, a motivated individual can still make a big difference. Chapter 10 speaks to building the personal strength to step forward.

Personal notes and ideas

Examples for my industry

Examples from other industries

Potential good questions

Personal Growth, Quantum Thinking and Planning

ONE OF THE THINGS I ENJOYED MOST about working with my colleagues at GBN was the opportunity to exchange war stories from
consulting engagements. One story that I remember vividly was told
by Peter Schwartz, chairman of GBN, with absolute amazement in
his voice. He was leading a senior group of managers at a high-tech
firm in a scenario planning and strategy development process. It was
an all-day meeting with lots of preparation and well-focused material to help analyze some big decisions. The meeting had been under
way for a couple of hours when one senior manager decided that
he would no longer participate because he did not agree with the
others. He then proceeded to turn his chair around so that his back
faced the group, and he sat in this position for well over an hour.
He did this despite the fact that the CEO of his company was in the
meeting observing his behavior. (This person left the company within
a year of the incident.)

This was surely the most blatant undermining personal behavior I have ever heard about during a planning meeting, but I have experienced more subtle and almost as destructive behaviors that damage the ability of people to think creatively and openly. Behaviors that indicate disrespect (eye rolling, ignoring the speaker, showing signs of impatience, and cutting people off while speaking) are very typical. Behaviors that indicate privilege are also very common (dominating the conversation, "correcting" others, and verbally enforcing "order"). An underlying context of "Get to the bottom line, we are in a hurry, and do it fast" also pervades a lot of planning meetings. There are all kinds of behaviors that stifle openness and creative thinking.

Who You Are and Good Planning

Why do people do mean things to each other? What is going on inside of us that leads us to treat other human beings so disrespectfully? How do we change this kind of damaging behavior? At the core, I believe, is a misplaced notion of who we are, or who this "I" is that we see ourselves as. Eckhart Tolle marks this idea in *A New Earth: Awakening to Your Life's Purpose* .

THE ILLUSORY SELF

The word "I" embodies the greatest error and the deepest truth, depending on how it is used. In conventional usage, it is not only one of the most frequently used words in the language (together with the related words: "me," "my," "mine," and "myself") but also one of the most misleading. In normal everyday usage, "I" embodies the primordial error, a misperception of who you are, an illusory sense of identity. This is the ego. This illusory sense of self is what Albert Einstein, who had deep insights not only into the reality of time and space, but also human nature, referred

*to as "an optical illusion of consciousness." That illusory self
then becomes the basis for all further interpretation or rather
misinterpretation of reality, of thought processes, interactions and
relationships.*

Holding and using the quantum-planning ideas will not be easy,
especially for people who have slipped into thinking of an all-powerful
"I." The quantum ideas are an acid test for how open one can be.
Holding and using quantum ideas will run up against negative and
limiting internal beliefs and trigger psychological pushback from people
committed to protecting those beliefs because they are "theirs." If you
are accustomed to dualistic thinking and rely on it to see yourself as
knowledgeable and intelligent, then you will certainly face some challenges in accepting and implementing these ideas. Removing and minimizing dualistic thinking will be required. In social situations, where
you now rely on dualistic analysis, you will have to be more reflective
and open. You may even have to deal with people you don't like to get
a really diverse point of view. As you have been reading this book, the
book has also been reading you. Your ability to stay open to the ideas
or close them down has set up a feedback loop in your subconscious.
If you don't resist, then the ideas are not finished with you yet and can
resurface in ways that lead to more creative thoughts.

You and Your Colleagues Are the Strategic Plan

In the case of the fellow who turned his back to his colleagues, it was
very clear he had personal problems. They could include immaturity,
communication challenges, disrespect for others, and poor teamwork
(interestingly enough, this person had risen to a very high position in

the company despite those bad habits). But imagine the energy wasted by his actions and the energy that needed to be expended following the meeting. I can imagine the political dynamics released in the organization between those who agreed with him and those who didn't. His eventual departure, despite his shortcomings, cost the company a significant investment in a high-level employee. It probably also limited the effectiveness of both the leadership and the strategic planning process.

Eckhart Tolle makes a great point in his writings about the only time being now—this very moment. Taking this point to heart, it is clear that once a plan is put together by the work of a leadership team, and all of the research, thinking, scenario-creation and options-analysis is done, implementation is done in the now. The words on the page of plan don't do the acting. Actions are taken by people in the real world, which hardly ever conforms to the assumptions and expectations driving the plan. Therefore the leadership team must implement the plan by learning forward and communicating in real time in the present moment. The people in the ongoing real-time process of learning forward, communicating, directing action and cooperating are essential to the strategic plan. They are one and the same—the people are the plan, you and your group are the plan.

Making Your Contribution

I have discovered that a good sign that indicates you are on a good personal track when involved in a planning process is your ability to play. It almost sounds like going back to kindergarten, but learning by having an open and somewhat playful attitude opens up space for creativity, sharing ideas, and treating others with kindness and respect. If you are too serious (or metaphorically like me in my golf lesson, holding the club too tightly), it is a signal to do a little self-checking and personal reflection.

I encourage planners to take more risks: be creative and use the seven quantum ideas presented in this book as ways to open up thinking. The process becomes personal when taking those risks brings up fears or triggers confusion, discomfort, or resentment. Personal transformation is possible when those fears and feeling of discomfort are looked at and seen as not real, but as illusions of the ego. The fears and feeling of discomfort are not perfect reflections of reality and can be disarmed through reflection. Rollo May puts it this way in his book *Man's Search for Himself.*

> *Consciousness of self gives us the power to stand outside the rigid chain of stimulus and response, to pause, and by this pause, throw some weight on either side, to cast some decision about what the response will be.*

There is a direct connection between our ability to do this as individuals and our ability to do it in organizations. Our organizations are nothing but collections of people. Reflective thinking and staying out of reactivity based on fear and discomfort directly connect with the ability to think creatively and openly in a planning process. The dysfunction of a team of planners is the sum of the dysfunction of the individual team members. The dysfunction of the lead planner (for example, the CEO) reflects down to dysfunction in the organization below him or her. You need only to read the newspaper stories of the colossal collapses of huge companies to see ample evidence of this.

I think two actions can reduce how personal dysfunction harms planning activities.

1. Learn and use reflective thinking while doing planning. If possible, formally incorporate it into the planning process by

setting aside time to challenge assumptions and vital beliefs and to consider outliers. If it can't be done formally in the process, you as a participant can do it personally and bring your contributions back into the group process.

2. Understand and do not underestimate how the limitations of your own personal development are playing a large role in the planning activities you are involved in.

Reflective Thinking and Playing with Quantum Ideas

I think it is only fair that, as I have asked you to be courageous and play with the quantum ideas and think reflectively, I give you some hints at how to get started. I think a good way is to pull key invigorating questions from the seven quantum ideas that can trigger reflective thinking. Figure 3 contains what I feel can be good kick-off questions for each of the seven quantum ideas. Feel free to add your own.

Creating the Learning Agenda to Keep the Plan "Off the Shelf"

During planning, a good question is often of equal or higher importance than the answer. It is in this spirit that I am encouraging you to use the quantum ideas in your thinking, planning, and learning your way forward. Some stones have to be overturned to see what lies beneath. Some sacred cows have to be gorged. To really institute learning-oriented strategy, you will have to push your thinking and work hard to find good questions. To help you formulate good questions while doing your planning, here are ten general questions that can be addressed to your organization. The list can serve as the basis from which you can create your own specific learning agenda relevant

---

FIGURE 3

REFLECTIVE THINKING AND QUANTUM IDEAS

Quantum Idea	Questions to Trigger Reflective Thinking
Thinking Beyond Duality	Where are we holding onto a position too tightly? What might we see if we were to shift our position on something we see as vital? Where am I holding on to an idea because it is mine?
Inescapable Uncertainty	What is it that we think we "know" but may actually have no real proof is true? Where might a connection between factors and feedback loops cause change?
Intentions, Actions, and Reality	Can a shift in my point of view help me see something new and different? Does what we say it is determine what it is? Could it evolve into something else?
Space, Time, Things, and Order	Where are we locked in and depending on a "before-and-after" way of seeing things? What new thing might happen that could change the order of our thinking?
Catalytic and Kaleidoscopic	What might change the whole picture from our perspective? What little things might cause big changes?
Field of All Possibilities	What are we (am I) believing is impossible that might have a huge impact? How might our own actions feed back into our plans and strategy?
Organizations As Energy Systems	How are our ideas and the value we are seeking to deliver working together? What might be changing in what our customers find valuable that could energize demand?

to your organization and the context of your planning. Be sure not to shy away from questions that make people uncomfortable.

Once you have settled on a good set of questions, formalize them as the learning agenda that will continue the strategic conversation of the organization. Gather a group of champions from across the organization (even some volunteers, if necessary) who will "own" those questions. Senior leadership of the organization should endorse this group and expect to get informal and periodic reports. This group should meet (short meetings are fine, even over lunch) regularly to share what they are learning and what, if any, implications they see for the organization. This material will become the "fertile" ground from which the next planning cycle will emerge. It also serves as useful material for comparisons against the uncertainties and core ideas of the old plan. This process will keep the organization in a proactive planning stance.

I will end this chapter with a quote from William James that might inspire you.

Genius, in truth, means little more than the
faculty of perceiving in an unhabitual way.

Ten Questions to Help Create More Questions for Your Learning Agenda

1. Are we looking at the organization as if it were a static, disconnected thing and not as a living system with energy?

2. Do we perceive something (an asset, resource, or product) too narrowly, as maybe being only one thing when it could be more?

3. What if a different set of values were being applied to our position? What might we learn or see differently?

4. What do we think is unknowable, and how will we find and use diverse points of view about it?

5. How can we see this beyond a "right hand versus left hand" perspective and look for the "top and bottom, front and back, in and out, and all around"?

6. What are our real intentions, and if we changed them, what would we see differently and need to learn more about?

7. Where is a sequence of events vital to our thinking? If the sequence were broken, how would we capture what we might learn?

8. What is on the periphery of our concerns that could change and become central, and how can we efficiently learn more about it?

9. How might we evolve and change in a manner that incorporates what we have done in the past with new elements that take us to a new level?

10. How can we see ourselves through the eyes of others (competitors, customers, regulators, and organizations in adjacent markets) and learn from those perspectives?

Personal notes and ideas

Examples for my industry

Examples from other industries

Potential good questions

Change, Creativity, and Innovation

SO WHAT OVERARCHING THOUGHTS do I have from working with the seven ideas presented in this book? Having worked with them for several years now, I find they have influenced how I think about change and creativity, and how change and creativity relate. In quantum physics there is an explanation of how the invisible becomes the visible, and changing states of energy suddenly move from what seems like nothing to something.

Rethinking Creativity

My discussion about changing perspectives and making what was not there before seem apparent has parallels in physics. Think of something vibrating invisibily at a very high level, then slowing its vibration level, and suddenly becoming visible. An example we see every day is how

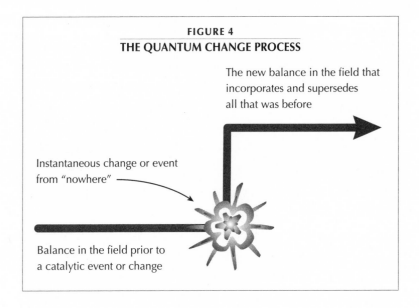

FIGURE 4
THE QUANTUM CHANGE PROCESS

The new balance in the field that incorporates and supersedes all that was before

Instantaneous change or event from "nowhere"

Balance in the field prior to a catalytic event or change

water vapor encountering lower temperatures (less vibration) moves from gas to liquid to solid (ice). If we were to imagine water vapor as having a mind, we could assume that it might never imagine itself as an ice cube. But something happens in the field (the temperature drops) and lo and behold, that water is now an ice cube. The ice cube is still water, but it now has different features and properties from water vapor. (Another way to think about this kind of transformation is in evolution, which is a slower biological process where the appearance of a new gene can cause a state change.) Figure 4 broadly illustrates this process.

What I see illustrated is a system in balance until something new enters, which causes change and then rebalancing. The change can be either a shift in the broader environment or an exogenous catalytic event. As one or more components in the system interact with and process (or integrate) this new thing, creative ideas begin to flow, and, through their expression, balance is reestablished. This is often how evolution is explained. I see this process as translatable to defining creativity in how our organizations adjust to change. Strategic planning sets the direction of our organizations into the uncertain future. The future we know will be full of change. The nature of the change can vary widely, among the most important possibilities being shifting economic conditions, technological change, new customer demand and values, and new laws and regulations. These changes can come from "nowhere." They can be systemic in nature or a catalytic "bang!"

Actually, I don't see that change in human events comes from "nowhere." It just seems that way. I think change in human events parallels the process in physics: something vibrating at a higher level slows down and becomes visible and "real." There is an emergent quality. The higher vibration and unseen places from which new things emerge are in the unconscious and subconscious minds of people (again think of music). A new idea or a new invention emerges from the human mind, often after some period of gestation where it has been hiding while being shaped and mulled over. All of a sudden, aha! Someone gets a new idea, is able to express a new demand or desire, or sees a possibility previously unseen. The invisible is now on its way to becoming visible. Something from the mind can now begin to crystallize. Human energy, drive, and ingenuity will be applied to turn it into reality. This is the beginning of the creative process. Once the process gathers momentum, the rest of the world will have to adjust to it. We must all now incorporate and integrate this new thing, and shift to a new balance in the field of all possibilities. As we do so, subsequent waves of creativity follow the appearance of "something emerging from nowhere." Figure 5 reinterprets Figure 4 for organizations.

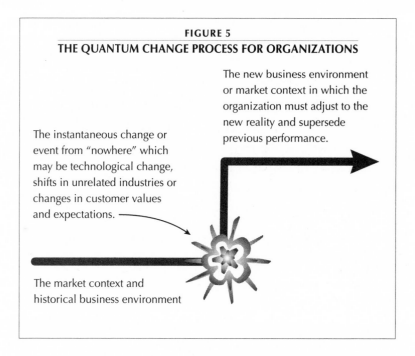

FIGURE 5
THE QUANTUM CHANGE PROCESS FOR ORGANIZATIONS

The new business environment or market context in which the organization must adjust to the new reality and supersede previous performance.

The instantaneous change or event from "nowhere" which may be technological change, shifts in unrelated industries or changes in customer values and expectations.

The market context and historical business environment

I think the innovation driven by the emergence of the Internet and low-cost global communications is an example of this kind of large quantum transformation in all of our lives and society as a whole. The communications revolution is causing a quantum shift at the level of industries as well; consider what it is doing in industries such as newspapers and advertising. There is a multi-media transformation occurring in how, when and where consumers get daily information and how we buy and sell products and services. Despite the pain in those changes for companies who are not able to adapt, I see the net effects as being positive and adding more flexibility, choice, and ways to connect people with what they want.

I believe this kind of creative transformation is bound to continue in the future and emerge from the following places, among others.

1. Biotechnology as it changes medicine, health, and knowledge about the human body and life extension.

2. Nanotechnology as it allows the creation of new materials with fantastic new properties in strength, flexibility, weight, and electrical resistance, among others.

3. Digital technologies as memory, computing power, and software capabilities continue to combine in delivering new communications, information processingl, and personal service applications.

4. The rise in political and economic power in Asia and developing countries in general, especially with their younger populations.

5. A growing acceptance of human and cultural diversity with people reaching across ethnic and others dividing lines toward judging others based on talent and ability (communications technology will accelerate what I believe to be this long-term historical trend).

6. Changes in the natural environment as global climate change affects where we live, grow our food, and have access to abundant fresh water resources (in particular, moving past tipping points in which reversing damage or changes is not possible).

For planners, I believe understanding creativity in this manner will give support to planning as learning, as adapting, and for holding a place for consistent interaction with a changing world. The seven ideas can, in turn, serve as tools through which to see the change and begin to create new products, services, and organizations. The seven ideas can help in creating new models and metaphors upon which plans and actions can be shared.

OK, I have given you my best shot. I have put forth the notion that some of the basic ideas of quantum physics can have broader applications in our world—that they can lead us to new ways of thinking, planning for, and thus creating new kinds of organizations. I am challenging people who plan the future of their organizations to think differently and to use the tools I have discussed as an aid. You now have scientifically verifiable tools to resist groupthink, oversimplification, and imagination-killing behaviors.

The core of what I am arguing for in using my quantum planning ideas is to recognize the connection between the outside-in and the inside-out of strategic planning. Strategic planning, as it manages uncertainty, focuses a lot on the outside forces that shape the business environment and that are mostly beyond our control. Metaphysics on the other hand focuses on the inside-out of the creative process. It is what we see in our mind's eye, feel in our hearts, and direct our intention to in order to tap into the key creative spark from which all flows. What I have argued is that strategic planning and metaphysics are intimately connected and that both head and heart must be used in good planning. Strategic planning and metaphysics combine in the mind and in the thinking process of the planner. The two can connect to energy in the heart to draw on perseverance (maybe even faith). My intention in discussing the quantum ideas is to show that they have something to contribute to both mind and heart. For the mind, quantum planning offers new metaphors and models for how reality might emerge. For the heart, quantum planning asserts that the very structure of the universe can be used to create new kinds of organizations that allow us to meet needs and desires that can be released through our infinite imaginations.

Scenario Planning and Applying Quantum Planning

AFTER HAVING PARTICIPATED IN over 100 scenario planning projects during my career, I hope that writing this book advances the practice of scenario development a few notches. I will explain here ways to get more value out of scenario-based planning through incorporation of the quantum ideas I have discussed.

As a reminder (and for readers who are not familiar with scenario planning), the core steps in a scenario-planning process are as follows.

1. Get a clear idea of what you need to assess for future developments that will impact the organization (e.g., the future of related technology developments, market trends or economic developments). Be clear on what you are uncertain about.

2. Create the group of people (insiders, outsiders, key experts) you need involved in the scenario-development process.

3. Use a good process or a capable facilitator to help create scenarios that are diverse and challenging and that are based on key factors that will influence future developments in the area you are uncertain about. Include any predetermined elements you can identify as well.

4. If there is a desire, perform some quantitative analyses based on the scenarios to calibrate impacts on financial, economic, and key performance measures.

5. Use the scenarios as thinking devices to create options for strategic actions. Existing strategies may be tested in the context of the scenarios, or other thinking devices can be used to create strategic options (for example, the competitive structure of the industry you are in can be "wind-tunneled" through the scenarios by assessing how different business conditions might lead to different competitive actions by existing companies and potential new entrants).

6. Isolate the strategic options that are robust across the scenarios, and move them toward internal management processes for further assessment and action planning. Isolate strategic options that are contingent upon certain scenarios. Decide whether to pursue those contingent options based on the organization's appetite for risk. Early indicators for events that might be favorable for pursuing those contingent options can also be researched, allowing those options to be "put on the shelf, but ready." This adds a proactive element to strategic planning. Early indicators can also be a key part of the learning-forward agenda.

Good scenarios can serve as the center of learning-oriented planning, as the steps in creating scenarios and using their outputs lead to new ideas and innovation. Learning opportunities and innovative thinking in the scenario process can emerge at the following stages.

1. When brainstorming and researching the forces and trends in the business environment of the organization, do it in an open fashion. Take note of information that is unusual or contrary to current views in the organization. Important issues that seem to defy a clear analysis should be put on a learning agenda.

2. When the central arguments and logical progression of a set of scenario stories are settled on, create a flowchart description of each one. Use the flowcharts over time as events unfold as a check against real and expected events. Notice and discuss trends or events that are outside the set of scenarios. Assess what they may mean for any key strategies.

3. Settle on at least two early indicators that could be associated with the set of contingent strategic options that emerged from the scenarios to the strategy process. These early indicators will be changing trends or events that can have a positive, negative, or unexpected influence on contingent strategic options. Lessons and insights from this process can be especially useful in seeing risks and opportunities for the organization.

Scenarios are stories with plots (the better the plots in explaining the logical progression of the scenario, the better the outcome). The plot lines are often archetypes (a journey, winners and losers, revolution, etc.). Plot lines are important because they make the stories in the scenarios comprehensible by touching on ideas already in people's minds.

What I have experienced over the years as a scenario planner is a consistent conservative thread in scenarios driven by a lack of creativity in the plot lines of the stories. In some cases the plot lines limit thinking and the ability of planners to be creative—there is not enough flexibility in imagining how events may develop.

Limited frames and metaphors can actually lead to limited thinking and skewed views of reality. Expanded frames and new metaphors can give us new ways from which to view and assess reality and reduce the hidden bias driven by old frames and metaphors. The seven quantum ideas I have discussed, I believe, can provide new plot lines and thus new viewpoints for thinking, learning, and planning. Incorporating these ideas into scenario-planning processes will expand thinking and strategy development by suggesting new avenues through which events might occur and opportunities may arise. Figure 6 provides ideas about how quantum thinking can be applied to the scenario-planning process.

Quantum Thinking and Business Structure

A key step in creating strategic options for a company once a good set of scenarios is in place is to "wind-tunnel" the business structure of the company or organization through the set of scenarios. This wind-tunneling through the scenarios can help planners see where there might be areas of stress, missing capabilities, or upside possibilities based on the strengths or weaknesses of the organization's structure. For a good way of thinking about business structure, see Kees van der Heijden's book, *The Art of Strategic Conversation,* and his concept of the business idea of the organization, which reveals through a flow diagram the core economics, value flows, and competitive advantage of the organization). Because of the capabilities of communications

FIGURE 6
QUANTUM IDEAS AND SCENARIO THINKING

Thinking Beyond Duality	Create scenarios in which identical events lead to very different results. Assess the implications of scenarios from multiple points of view, including competitors, regulators, or other key stakeholders, to expand strategy development.
Inescapable Uncertainty	Create scenarios with plot lines in which perceptions about an industry and actions from those outside of it or peripheral to it are driving change.
Intentions, Actions, and Reality	Create consumer-centric scenarios with plot lines in which consumers and outside forces redefine the market dynamics of a product or service.
Space, Time, Things, and Order	Create scenarios that allow wide flexibility in the life cycle of a product or service with sustainable interactions between producers and consumers.
Catalytic and Kaleidoscopic	Create wild card scenarios where catalytic and kaleidoscopic events drive plot lines. Look for early indicators that may signal catalytic potential. Create strategic options that can be catalytic.
Field of All Possibilities	Utilize the concept of the balance of forces in scenario development, where there are plots of market forces moving out of and into balance, and what can happen at the extremes.
Organizations As Energy Systems	In the strategy development process, see the company or organization as a living system, not just as a financial entity. Isolate which factors contribute to its life force, and create strategies to sustain it.

technology in today's world (the Internet and emerging uses of radio frequency identity technology in particular), I believe that humankind is entering an era where we can create quantum structured organizations. I see Wikipedia and YouTube as precursors to what will be an explosion of creativity similar to the impact on business formation of the interstate highway system in the U.S. We are building through our communications, computers, and network systems a new form of infrastructure, and one of the benefits will be organizations that can take advantage of quantum principles in their structure. The key capability that these organizations will utilize is interconnectivity and the ability to connect all (in particular, all people and, eventually, probably all machines) to all. The connection of all to all will create an energy system in which ideas will flow that will allow people to reconfigure physical assets and their uses to better serve our needs. An "economics of coordination" will be enabled by communications infrastructure and interconnectivity. The economics of coordination will drive down costs by removing wasted time and resources as people become able to make better decisions based on access to information. Quantum organizational structures for businesses and organizations will emerge from this process. (There are several books on the future of technology and society that suggest these ideas and more. Two of the best thinkers on this topic, in my opinion, are Manuel Castells, in his book *The Rise of Network Society,* and Joel Garreau, who points out the darker side in his book *Radical Evolution*). My thoughts about the structural elements that might appear in organizations that embody quantumlike structures are summarized in Figure 7.

Quantum ideas will help create quantum-structured businesses that will provide quantum leaps in service and products that will improve the human experience.

FIGURE 7

QUANTUM IDEAS AND BUSINESS STRUCTURE

Thinking Beyond Duality	Organizations will create products and services that have discrete and continuous forms, and they will support consumers in both modes.
Inescapable Uncertainty	Firms will intentionally create feature-rich products and services that have multiple capabilities with a purpose of serving very diverse consumer needs.
Intentions, Actions, and Reality	Companies will incorporate capabilities for consumers to participate directly in the design of products and services and incorporate a feedback loop for learning about alternative uses of their products and services.
Space, Time, Things, and Order	Companies will move toward a total-life-cycle approach to products and services and will design products and services that have a sustainability component.
Catalytic and Kaleidoscopic	Products and services will be designed with an openness that allows continuous change or enhancement by the customer and others. A learning feedback loop will capture the best of these open-access innovations.
Field of All Possibilities	A component of "allness" will be basic to product and service design, based on interconnectedness. "Allness" will be a way to connect production and consumption and to support high levels of service.
Organizations As Energy Systems	Organizations will be built that allow energy and ideas to move freely and quickly and allow the instant restructuring of a flexible base of assets (digital assets will be the most flexible)

An Example of Quantum Thinking and Strategy

Quantum thinking and strategy development as I am describing it means embedding a quantum idea into the structure of the company. Of course, because this is my language, I have not found a CEO who would parrot my words. Nevertheless, since I have made the recommendation, it is good for me to present an example from the real world. (For the full story see the Clive Thomson article "I'm So Totally, Digitally Close to You" in the September 7, 2008, issue of the *New York Times Sunday Magazine*. It describes a decision made by Mark Zuckerberg in the creation of a new feature, News Feed, on the Facebook.com web service. The News Feed feature was a convenience that allowed friends to get updates about the changes on a user's page. With this new feature, users and their friends would no longer need to spend time searching all their friends' pages for small or significant updates. When the service was initially launched, there was a negative reaction by Facebook.com users (up to 284,000 people joined a protest group). According to the story, Zuckerberg made two decisions. The first was to make some changes to the feature to allow more privacy, and the second was to stick to his first decision. What made the News Feed feature a quantum structure in my language is this: It allowed what the *Times* called, "omnipresent knowledge." And when users figured this out, according to the *Times*, they found it "intriguing and addictive." The author went on to describe the service as creating what social scientists call "ambient awareness," which he defined as "like being physically near someone and picking up on his mood through the little things he does—body language, sights, stray comments— out of the corner of your eye." The quantum aspects of this strategy fit perfectly with seeing the company as an energy system and the interconnectivity inherent in the field of all possibilities. I cannot put words or thoughts into Zuckerberg's mouth, but in my estimation, he was betting on a quantum structure holding up.

I believe there will be quantum-structured business beyond the digital realm and in the hard product realm when life-cycle thinking and sustainable designs become the norm. The process of all outputs becoming inputs into another process or product, with very little to no waste, will be a foundation of quantum business structures.

A Quantum Scenario for the Future of the Energy Sector

The energy business is ripe for the kind of quantum change I have been writing about. Below is my fictional quantum-transformation scenario for the future of the energy business. It is told from the point of view of a billionaire investor who led a venture fund and watched the whole thing unfold.

A Quantum Transformation Scenario
The Coming World of Zero-Price Energy

By Corbin Harris, Chairman of New Energy Ventures, Ltd.

When I graduated from the University of Chicago Graduate School of Business in 2008, I never imagined the direction my life was about to take. It all started during a couple of job interviews I had looking to kick off my career. The first was with Toyota Motor Company. Since my undergraduate degree was in Mechanical Engineering, they thought the Finance and Business Economics background I got with my MBA made me a good candidate. They drove me around in a 2009 Toyota Prius, which I thought was really slick. As an engineer I was really interested in the design of the car and found that the most interesting part of the discussion was on what was called "regenerative braking." It basically gathered wasted energy when the car was braking and used this to charge the batteries that gave the car its electric energy power. I thought this was interesting and recalled a mention of the research on the next generation of batteries for the vehicle and the likelihood of continuing innovation there. I recalled my father telling me (until I was tired of hearing it), "Son, there is no energy crisis or energy shortage, just bad technology. We waste a lot of energy and more energy strikes the earth every day than humanity uses in a year! We also have very poor energy storage technology. With a few breakthroughs the price of electricity should fall to zero." I used to think he was off his rocker with gasoline prices at over four dollars a gallon.

My second interview was with Intel, and of course I really wanted to work there. I envisioned always being on the cutting edge of technology working with such a company. Oddly enough I ran into the energy angle again there. They were just announcing a new approach to charging devices through something called "resonant magnetic field" charging. The technology was the brainchild of an MIT professor by the name of Marin Soljacic, who invented it as a way to transmit power wirelessly. With the new technology you could just place your computer on a desk and it would start charging itself. I did not get the Intel job but I did some searching around on this fellow Marin Soljacic and his technology.

Fortunately, I did get a job, as an analyst at a venture-fund company looking to invest in new energy technology. I decided to see if my dad was right and to find the companies to prove it. The fund already had some investment in the solar-cell industry and was beginning to look at battery systems. The batteries going into hybrid cars were providing some solid sales growth for the industry, and we expected this to continue.

I remember it like it was yesterday, the conversation I had with Dr. Gary May, a young graduate student from the Georgia Institute of Technology studying under Soljacic at MIT. In the summer of 2010, he said he could see a day when electricity would be the dominant form of energy used in the world (no pollution at the end point of use, and with wind power, solar, nuclear, and high-efficiency natural gas turbines for basic generation, pollution could be better managed at the generation stage). He also pointed out that with solar energy the fuel price is essentially zero. In the long run, once you recovered the fixed capital cost, then logically the marginal cost of electricity from solar energy would fall to zero. (Good economist, I thought.) The only thing you would be paying for was any customized uses that had special designs at the consumption point. He called this the "atomization of energy," meaning custom-designed energy depending on the value-added features desired by the consumer. What we couldn't see at the time was the key elements of the combined new energy system that would make his dream come true. I spent my career figuring this out and building the companies that would deliver on these promises.

In 2015 we got a big breakthrough in our thinking that made all the difference; it went back to the regenerative-braking idea. For decades many people rightfully argued that energy efficiency was vital and we had to stop wasting so much. During this year, an obscure research paper emerged from a group of scientists at the University of Chicago suggesting that a combination of solar power, efficient design, regeneration, and energy storage offered a way forward to a new energy system. It argued that efficiency alone was not enough, but capturing energy in regenerative systems would be an additional key element. The paper asked the question about regeneration: Why are we throwing away so much energy after we use it? The paper also argued for research on improved battery systems, where losses from charging and releasing energy would be reduced. The paper essentially started a research and development explosion. Early magnetic resonant power systems were also showing big improvement with each new generation of technology.

In 2018, we made our first big investment in what we called a "new energy services system company." It was our first move into custom energy systems that combined multiple technologies: solar, battery storage, nascent regeneration, and custom designs at each point of energy use. Our energy services company would look at how a business was using energy (lighting, heat, powering light equipment or heavy machines with large torque) and we'd custom-design a whole energy system with multiple sources of power. We were not able to get completely off the power grid, but in most cases the grid represented less than 20 percent of our power usage. The energy technologies we were now working with to build our systems were coming from new companies that did not exist in 2012. One was an Intel spin-off (in which we were 50 percent owners) developing systems to broadcast resonant magnetic field power.

Innovation and sales growth in the hybrid-auto sector helped a lot when, starting in 2020, the plug-in hybrid vehicles were so good that most cars were getting well over 80 miles to a gallon of gasoline. Most people were finding that for 75 percent of their trips they could travel on electric power alone. They could also charge up at night for really low costs. The profits generated from the battery systems in these cars had funded an explosion of competition in the sector, and the companies were building energy-storage systems whose market reach extended far beyond the auto industry, especially tied with the now 50 percent–efficient solar-power systems. On even partly cloudy days, these systems could charge up a bank of batteries in 5 hours and provide continuous power.

In 2025, we advertised our first zero-priced power system. It was not exactly free, but what we offered was a combination of technology and financing so that within three years, most people who bought our system were paying nothing for their electric power. We calculated that with repayment of their loans, three-year depreciation of the investment in equipment, and solar power as the primary fuel, their electricity would be essentially free. We were able to back up this promise because each year our systems got better and cheaper. The technology innovation curve, driven by nanotechnology, advanced materials, and digital technology, provided cost-saving advancements on a regular basis.

The systems we were installing by 2030 are the ones that put the new energy system for the entire world firmly into place. By this time our regeneration options were expanding and the cost and efficiency of solar and battery storage systems were so much better that we could provide options for rural areas of developing countries. Our international investment propelled growth of the fund and made us proud not only of our returns to investors, but our ability to make the world a better place.

Bibliography

Al-Khalili, Jim. *Quantum, A Guide for the Perplexed.* London: Weidenfeld & Nicholson, Orion House, 2003

Allan, Julie, Gerard Fairtlough, and Barbara Heinzen. *The Power of the Tale: Using Narratives for Organisational Success.* West Sussex, England: Wiley, 2002.

Campbell, Joseph. *The Inner Reaches of Outer Space: Metaphor as Myth as Religion.* Novato, CA: New World Library, 1986.

Castells, Manuel. *The Rise of Network Society: The Information Age: Economy, Society, Culture, Volume 1.* Cambridge: Blackwell, 1996, 1998, and 2000.

Christensen, Clayton M. *The Innovator's Dilemma: When New Technologies Cause Great Firms to Fail.* Boston: Harvard Business School Press, 1997.

"Confessions of a Risk Manager." *The Economist,* vol. 388, no. 8592, August 9–15, 2008, 72–73.

De Martino, Benedetto, Dharshan Kumaran, Ben Seymour, and Raymond J. Dolan. "Frames, Biases and Rational Decision Making in the Human Brain." *Science Magazine,* vol. 313, August 4, 2006, 684–687.

Frankl, Viktor E. *Man's Search for Meaning,* revised and updated. New York: Washington Square Press, 1984.

Garreau, Joel. *Radical Evolution: The Promise and Peril of Enhancing Our Minds, Our Bodies—And What It Means to Be Human.* New York: Doubleday, 2005.

de Geus, Arie. *The Living Company: Habits for Survival in a Turbulent Business Environment,* Boston: Harvard Business School Press, 1997.

———. "Planning as Learning." Boston: *Harvard Business Review,* March–April 1988.

Hawkins, David R., MD, PhD. *The Eye of the I: From Which Nothing Is Hidden.* West Sedona, AZ: Veritas Publishing, second printing revised 2002.

Hill, Napoleon. *Think & Grow Rich.* New York: Fawcett Crest, 1960.

Isaacson, Walter. *Einstein: His Life and Universe.* New York, Simon and Schuster, 2007.

Krishnamurti, J. *Freedom from the Known.* San Francisco: HarperSanFrancisco, 1969.

Lakoff, George. *Don't Think of an Elephant: Know Your Values and Frame the Debate.* White River Junction, VT: Chelsea Green Publishing, 2004.

Lewis, Thomas, MD, Fari Amini, MD, Richard Lannon, MD. *A General Theory of Love.* New York: Random House, 2000.

Lowenstein, Roger. *When Genius Failed: The Rise and Fall of Long-Term Capital Management.* New York: Random House, 2000.

Markoff, John. "Intel Moves to Free Gadgets of Their Charging Cords." *New York Times,* August 20, 2008.

May, Rollo. *Man's Search for Himself.* New York: Dell Publishing, 1973.

Schwartz, Peter. *The Art of the Long View: Planning for the Future in an Uncertain World.* New York: Doubleday, 1991.

Soros, George. *The Alchemy of Finance: Reading the Mind of the Market.* New York: Simon and Schuster, 1987.

———. *The Crisis of Global Capitalism: Open Society Endangered.* New York: Public Affairs, 1998.

Thompson, Clive. "I'm So Totally, Digitally Close to You." *New York Times Sunday Magazine,* September 7, 2008, 42–47.

Tolle, Eckhart. *A New Earth: Awakening to Your Life's Purpose.* New York: Plume, 2005.

Van der Heijden, Kees. *Scenarios; The Art of Strategic Conversation.* Chichester, England: Wiley, 2005.

Van Natta, Don, Jr. and Alex Berenson. "ENRON Chairman Received Warnings About Accounting." *New York Times,* January 15, 2002.

If you want to know more about quantum physics, these are the books I found most interesting.

Goswami, Amit, with Richard Reed and Maggie Goswami. *The Self-Aware Universe: How Consciousness Creates the Material World* New York: Putnam, 1995.

Kaku, Michio. *Physics of the Impossible: A Scientific Exploration into the World of Phasers, Force Fields, Teleportation and Time Travel.* New York: Random House and Doubleday, 2008.

Moring, Gary F. *The Complete Idiot's Guide to Theories of the Universe.* New York: Penguin 2002.

Rae, Alastair I. M. *Quantum Physics: A Beginner's Guide. ,* Oxford, England: Oneworld, 2005.

Doing a quick review on Wikipedia.com of the listing under physics is also a good way to jump-start your understanding.

About the Author

AFTER GRADUATION FROM THE University of Chicago Graduate School of Business (recently renamed the Booth Graduate School of Business), Gerald Harris began his professional career in the investments and economics department at Bechtel Corporation where he assisted in arranging international project financing for energy plants. He then joined the corporate finance group at Pacific Gas and Electric (PG&E) to focus on the company's asset-based finance. After several years in the corporate finance group he was tapped to be part of the initial corporate planning department at PG&E and was subsequently promoted to be the director of planning for the engineering and construction division of the company. It was with this initial corporate experience that Gerald got a hands-on feel for strategic planning. After a 13-year career at PG&E, Gerald joined Global Business Network (GBN) to expand his strategic planning experience as a consultant working internationally. He mastered the scenario-planning process while at GBN, and over his 15-year career there, worked with many companies in the energy, mining, engineering, telecommunications, and information-technology industries, leading and facilitating company teams in developing scenarios and related strategies. He also led scenario-planning and strategy-development projects for government agencies and foundations in the public policy arena, in particular focusing on public education and economic development. Gerald thus understands strategic planning from both the internal company perspective and that of an external consultant. In 2008, Gerald became a member of the GBN's network of experts and contributors, and started to build his own consulting practice and team. More information is available at www.artofquantumplanning.com.

Index

Action/actions
    context connection, 47–49
    and continued learning, 93
    and intention, 28
    in real world/real time, 117
Aim-Control-Ready-Fire (ACRF)
    approach. *See* Field of all
    possibilities
Aim-Ready-Fire-Aim (ARFA)
    approach. *See* Field of all
    possibilities
The Alchemy of Finance (Soros),
    47–48
Allan, Julie, 80
Apple (computer company), 60,
    108
Arbitrary selectivity, 34. *See also*
    Dualistic thinking
Archetypes, and worldview, 18–19
The Art of Strategic Conversation
    (Heijden), 133
Assets, and ideas, 107–109
Atoms, concept of, 23

The Balanced Scorecard (Kaplan
    and Norton), 95
Balanced scorecard, in planning,
    95, 95*f*
Balance/out-of-balance situations, 87
Bank of America, 37
Banks, Ernie, 59
Baseball, 59
Bias, in market prices, 47–48
"Big Bang" theory, 26
Black-Scholes model, 5
Bohm, David, 42, 44
Book
    personalization of, 84
    use of, 19–20
    website for, 86
Brainstorming, 80–81, 132
Breakthroughs, technological, 45,
    69–70
Business environment
    connection/interaction in, 86–87
    and mismanaged companies,
       9–10

About Berrett-Koehler Publishers

Berrett-Koehler is an independent publisher dedicated to an ambitious mission: Creating a World That Works for All.

We believe that to truly create a better world, action is needed at all levels—individual, organizational, and societal. At the individual level, our publications help people align their lives with their values and with their aspirations for a better world. At the organizational level, our publications promote progressive leadership and management practices, socially responsible approaches to business, and humane and effective organizations. At the societal level, our publications advance social and economic justice, shared prosperity, sustainability, and new solutions to national and global issues.

A major theme of our publications is "Opening Up New Space." They challenge conventional thinking, introduce new ideas, and foster positive change. Their common quest is changing the underlying beliefs, mindsets, institutions, and structures that keep generating the same cycles of problems, no matter who our leaders are or what improvement programs we adopt.

We strive to practice what we preach—to operate our publishing company in line with the ideas in our books. At the core of our approach is stewardship, which we define as a deep sense of responsibility to administer the company for the benefit of all of our "stakeholder" groups: authors, customers, employees, investors, service providers, and the communities and environment around us.

We are grateful to the thousands of readers, authors, and other friends of the company who consider themselves to be part of the "BK Community." We hope that you, too, will join us in our mission.

Be Connected

Visit Our Website

Go to www.bkconnection.com to read exclusive previews and excerpts of new books, find detailed information on all Berrett-Koehler titles and authors, browse subject-area libraries of books, and get special discounts.

Subscribe to Our Free E-Newsletter

Be the first to hear about new publications, special discount offers, exclusive articles, news about bestsellers, and more! Get on the list for our free e-newsletter by going to www.bkconnection.com.

Get Quantity Discounts

Berrett-Koehler books are available at quantity discounts for orders of ten or more copies. Please call us toll-free at (800) 929-2929 or email us at bkp.orders@aidcvt.com.

Host a Reading Group

For tips on how to form and carry on a book reading group in your workplace or community, see our website at www.bkconnection.com.

Join the BK Community

Thousands of readers of our books have become part of the "BK Community" by participating in events featuring our authors, reviewing draft manuscripts of forthcoming books, spreading the word about their favorite books, and supporting our publishing program in other ways. If you would like to join the BK Community, please contact us at bkcommunity@bkpub.com.